The Collected Poems of
AUDRE LORDE

The
Collected Poems of
AUDRE LORDE

W. W. NORTON & COMPANY

New York   London

For information about permission to reproduce selections from this book, write to
Permissions, W. W. Norton & Company, Inc., 500 Fifth Avenue, New York, NY 10110.

The text of this book is composed in Centaur, with the display set in Charlemagne
Composition by Innodata Corporation
Manufacturing by LSC Harrisonburg
Book design by Charlotte Staub

Library of Congress Cataloging-in-Publication Data

Lorde, Audre.
        [Poems]
        The collected poems of Audre Lorde.
            p.   cm.
        Includes bibliographical references and index.
        ISBN 0-393-04090-9
        I. Title.
        PS3562.075A17   1997
        811'.54—dc21   97-10878   CIP
        ISBN 0-393-31972-5 pbk.

W. W. Norton & Company, Inc.
500 Fifth Avenue, New York, N.Y. 10110
www.wwnorton.com

W. W. Norton & Company Ltd.
15 Carlisle Street, London W1D 3BS

19   20

CONTENTS

CABLES TO RAGE (1970)

FROM A LAND WHERE
OTHER PEOPLE LIVE (1973)

NEW YORK HEAD SHOP AND MUSEUM (1974)

COAL (1976)

BETWEEN OUR SELVES (1976)

THE BLACK UNICORN (1978)

(NEW POEMS FROM)
CHOSEN POEMS: OLD AND NEW (1982)

OUR DEAD BEHIND US (1986)

THE MARVELOUS
ARITHMETICS OF DISTANCE (1993)

EDITOR'S NOTE

This collection includes the complete poems from nine volumes of Audre Lorde's poetry: *The First Cities; Cables to rage; From a Land Where Other People Live: New York Head Shop and Museum; Coal; Between Our Selves; The Black Unicorn; Our Dead Behind Us;* and *The Marvelous Arithmetics of Distance 1987–1992.* Throughout her career, Audre Lorde would revise, retitle, and republish selected poems. Hence, sixteen of the twenty-four poems which appear in Audre Lorde's first poetry collection, *The First Cities,* were revised minimally by the author and collected in a later volume, *Coal.* Fourteen of the poems which appear in *Cables to rage* also appear, some in slightly different versions, in *Coal.* In 1976, Audre Lorde published a small volume titled *Between Our Selves.* All seven poems from that volume also appear in *The Black Unicorn* in slightly different form. We have chosen to publish these nine volumes of Audre Lorde's poetry in their entirety, and have strived to render them exactly as they appeared in each original publication; however, we have chosen not to include any graphics and line drawings which may have appeared in some volumes, and we made a handful of corrections to those errors which were clearly typographical or inadvertent. In 1982 Audre Lorde's *Chosen Poems: Old and New* was published. That volume consists of a selection of revised poems from Audre Lorde's earlier collections, as well as several new poems. In 1992 *Undersong: Chosen Poems Old and New, Revised,* a revision of *Chosen Poems: Old and New,* was published and is currently available. From that volume, we have chosen to collect only the new poems.

THE FIRST CITIES

(1968)

For Genevieve, Miriam, Clem,
no more words
For Marian, Neal, Ed,
different ones.

Memorial II

Genevieve
What are you seeing
In my mirror this morning
Peering out like a hungry bird
From behind my eyes
Are you seeking the shape of a girl
I have grown less and less to resemble
Or do you remember
I could never accept your face dying
I do not know you now
Surely your vision stayed stronger than mine
Genevieve tell me where dead girls
Wander after their summer.

I wish I could see you again
Far from me—even
Birdlike flying into the sun
Your eyes are blinding me Genevieve.

"I Die for All Mysterious Things"

The Hanged Man
Broken
By fire
Is
Neither
More Beautiful
Nor
Less
Sane.

A Family Resemblance

My sister has my hair my mouth my eyes
And I presume her trustless.
When she was young, and open to any fever
Wearing gold like a veil of fortune on her face,
She waited through each rain a dream of light.
But the sun came up
Burning our eyes like crystal
Bleaching the sky of promise and
My sister stood
Black, unblessed and unbelieving
Shivering in the first cold show of love.

I saw her gold become an arch
Where nightmare hunted
Down the porches
Of her restless nights.
Now through the echoes of denial
She walks a bleached side of reason
Secret now
My sister never waits,
Nor mourns the gold that wandered from her bed.

My sister has my tongue
And all my flesh unanswered
And I presume her trustless as a stone.

Coal

I
Is the total black, being spoken
From the earth's inside.
There are many kinds of open.
How a diamond comes into a knot of flame
How a sound comes into a word, coloured
By who pays what for speaking.

Some words are open
Like a diamond on glass windows
Singing out within the crash of passing sun
Then there are words like stapled wagers
In a perforated book—buy and sign and tear apart—
And come whatever wills all chances
The stub remains
An ill-pulled tooth with a ragged edge.
Some words live in my throat
Breeding like adders. Others know sun
Seeking like gypsies over my tongue
To explode through my lips
Like young sparrows bursting from shell.
Some words
Bedevil me.

Love is a word another kind of open—
As a diamond comes into a knot of flame
I am black because I come from the earth's inside
Take my word for jewel in your open light.

What My Child Learns of the Sea

What my child learns of the sea
Of the summer thunder
Of the bewildering riddle that hides at the vortex of spring
She will learn in my twilight
And childlike
Revise every autumn.

What my child learns
As her winters fall out of time
Ripened in my own body
To enter her eyes with first light.

This is why
More than blood,
Or the milk I have given
One day a strange girl will step
To the back of a mirror
Cutting my ropes
Of sea and thunder and sun.
Of the way she will taste her autumns
Toast-brittle, or warmer than sleep
And the words she will use for winter
I stand already condemned.

Now that I Am Forever with Child

How the days went
While you were blooming within me
I remember each upon each—
The swelling changed planes of my body—
And how you first fluttered, then jumped
And I thought it was my heart.

How the days wound down
And the turning of winter
I recall, with you growing heavy
Against the wind. I thought
Now her hands
Are formed, and her hair
Has started to curl
Now her teeth are done
Now she sneezes.
Then the seed opened.
I bore you one morning just before spring—
My head rang like a firey piston
My legs were towers between which
A new world was passing.

From then
I can only distinguish
One thread within running hours
You . . . flowing through selves
Toward you.

Bridge through My Windows

In curve scooped out and necklaced with light
Burst pearls stream down my outstretched arms to earth
Oh bridge my sister bless me before I sleep
Wild air is lengthening
And I am tried beyond strength or bearing
Over water.

We are each of us both shorelines
A left country where time suffices
And the right land
Where pearls roll into earth and spring up day.
Joined our bodies have passage into one
Without a merging
As this slim necklace anchored into night.

And while the we conspires to make secret its two eyes
We search each other's shore for some crossing home.

Second Spring

We have no passions left to love the spring
Who had suffered autumn as we did, alone
Walking through dominions of a browning laughter
Carrying our loneliness our loving and our grief.

How can we know another spring.
For there will come no flower where was fruit before
Now we have little use for spring's relentless seeking
Who walked the long, unquestioned path
Straight into autumn's arms
Who saw the summer passions wither
Into a leaf to hide our naked tears.

Earth is still sweet, for autumn teaches bearing
And new sun will warm our proud and cautious feet
But spring came once
And we have seen the road that led through summer
Beautiful and bright as clover on a hill
Become a vast appalling wilderness and rain
While we stood still, racked on the autumn's knowing
Binding cold love to us with the corners of her shroud.

Spring III

Spring is the harshest
Blurring the lines of choice
Until summer flesh
Swallows up all decision.

I remember after the harvest was over
When the thick sheaves were gone
And the bones of the gaunt trees
Uncovered
How the dying of autumn was too easy
To solve our loving.

Gemini

Moon minded the sun goes farther from us
Split into swirled days, smoked,
Unhungered
And no longer young.

All earth falls down
Like lost light, frightened out between my fingers.
Here at the end of night, our love is a burned out ocean—
A dry-worded brittle bed.
The roots, once nourished by the lost water
Cry out—"remind us!"—and the oyster world
Cries out its pearls like tears.

Was this the wild calling I heard in the long night past
Wrapped in a stone-closed house?
I wakened to moon and the sound-breached dark—
And thinking a new word spoken
Some promise made
Broke through the screaming night seeking a gateway out

But the night was dark
And love was a burning fence about my house.

To a Girl Who Knew What Side
Her Bread Was Buttered On

He, through the eyes of the first marauder
Saw her, catch of bright thunder, heaping
Tea and bread for her guardian dead
Crunching the nut-dry words they said
And (thinking the bones were sleeping)
He broke through the muffled afternoon
Calling an end to their ritual's tune
With lightning-like disorder:

Leave the bones, Love! Come away
From these summer breads with the flavour of hay—
Your guards can watch the shards of our catch
Warming *our* bones on some winter's day!

Like an ocean of straws the old bones rose
Fearing the lightning's second death.
There was little time to wonder
At the silence of bright thunder
As, with a smile of pity and stealth
She buttered fresh scones for her guardian bones
And they trampled him into the earth.

Nightstone

No man is robbed of stone, of a dead root
Nor of losing
Though the rubbery mouth shouts
Through nights thickness "Stop—Thief—"
Only hope cobbles this thin remembering.
Brushing a thief's print from my doorway
I would wake
Trapped between a new day's smell
And the artful manner of you
Smoothing your skirt, or sneezing.

Dreaming, I walked fleshless
Through a robber's crying
—If you make me stone
I shall bruise you!
And the scent of your body withers
Into morning.

Stone remains
Holding me from the blasphemies
Of hunger.

Father Son and Holy Ghost

I have not ever seen my fathers grave.
Not that his judgment eyes have been forgotten
Nor his great hands print
On our evening doorknobs
One half turn each night and he would come
Misty from the worlds business
Massive and silent as the whole day's wish, ready
To re-define each of our shapes—
But that now the evening doorknobs
Wait, and do not recognize us as we pass.

Each week a different woman
Regular as his one quick glass each evening—
Pulls up the grass his stillness grows
Calling it weed. Each week
A different woman has my mother's face
And he, who time has
Changeless
Must be amazed, who knew and loved but one.

My father died in silence, loving creation
And well-defined response.
He lived still judgments on familiar things
And died, knowing a January fifteenth that year me.

Lest I go into dust
I have not ever seen my father's grave.

Pirouette

     I saw
Your hands on my lips like blind needles
Blunted
From sewing up stone
And
      Where are you from
                     you said
Your hands reading over my lips for
Some road through uncertain night
For your feet to examine home
      Where are you from
                     you said

Your hands
On my lips like thunder
Promising rain;
      A land where all lovers are mute.
And
      Why are you weeping
                     you said
Your hands on my doorway like rainbows
Following rain
Why are you weeping?

     I am come home.

Generation

How the young attempt and are broken
Differs from age to age
We were brown free girls
Love singing beneath their skin
Sun in their hair in their eyes
Sun their fortune
The taste of their young boys' manhood
Swelling like birds in their mouths.

In a careless season of power
We wept out our terrible promise
Now these are the children we try
For temptations that wear our face
And who came back from the latched cities of falsehood
Warning—the road to Nowhere is slippery with our blood
Warning—You need not drink the river to get home
For we purchased bridges with our mothers' bloody gold
We are more than kin who come to share
Not blood, but the bloodiness of failure.

How the young are tempted and betrayed
To slaughter or conformity
Is a turn of the mirror
Time's question only.

Echo

I hear myself drought caught
Pleading a windy cause
Dry as the earth without rain
Crying love, in tongues of false thunder
While my love waits
Like a seeded trap in the door of my house
Mouth bound with perfect teeth
Sure of their strength on bone
While my love waits
To swallow me whole
And pass me as echos of shadowless laughter
Quiet
My love
Waits at the door of my house.

In my yard myths of rain
Hang like a sheet of brick-caught silk
Torn in the sun.

Oaxaca

Beneath the carving drag of wood
The land moves slowly.
But lightning comes.

Growing their secret in brown earth
Spread like a woman
Daring
Is weary work for still-eyed men
Who break the earth, nurse their seed,
And a hard watching through the dry season.
Yet, at the edge of bright, thin day—
Past the split plow—they look
To the hills—to the brewing thunder
For the storm is known.

The land moves slowly.
Though the thunder's eye
Can crack with a flash
The glass-brittle crust of a mountain's face,
The land moves slowly.
All a man's strength and in his son's arms
To carve one sleeve into rock-defiant earth
And the spread land waits.

Slow, long, the plowing
Through dry-season brown,
And the land moves slowly.

But lightning comes.

Father, the Year Is Fallen

Father, the year is fallen.
Leaves bedeck my careful flesh like stone.
One shard of brilliant summer pierced me
And remains.
By this only,—unregenerate bone
I am not dead, but waiting.
When the last warmth is gone
I shall bear in the snow.

If You Come Softly

If you come as softly
As wind within the trees
You may hear what I hear
See what sorrow sees.

If you come as lightly
As threading dew
I will take you gladly
Nor ask more of you.

You may sit beside me
Silent as a breath
Only those who stay dead
Shall remember death.

And if you come I will be silent
Nor speak harsh words to you.
I will not ask you why, now.
Or how, or what you do.

We shall sit here, softly
Beneath two different years
And the rich earth between us
Shall drink our tears.

Suffer the Children

Pity for him who suffers from his waste.
Water that flows from the earth
For lack of roots to hold it
And children who are murdered
Before their lives begin.
Who pays his crops to the sun
When the fields are parched by drought
Will mourn the lost water while waiting another rain.
But who shall dis-inter these girls
To love the women they were to become
Or read the legends written beneath their skin?

Those who loved them remember their child's laughter.
But he whose hate has robbed him of their good
Has yet to weep at night above their graves.

Years roll out and rain shall come again.
But however many girls be brought to sun
Someday
A man will thirst for sleep in his southern night
Seeking his peace where no peace is
And come to mourn these children
Given to the dust.

A Child Shall Lead

I have a child
Whose feet are blind
On every road
But silence.

My boy has
Lovely foolish lips
But cannot find
His way to sun

And I am grown
Past knowledge.

A Lover's Song

Give me fire and I will sing you morning
Finding you heart
And a birth of fruit
For you, a flame that will stay beauty
Song will take us by the hand
And lead us back to light.

Give me fire and I will sing you evening
Asking you water
And quick breath
No farewell winds like a willow switch
Against my body
But a voice to speak
In a dark room.

Return

You did not clock the falling of the leaves
The silent turning of the grass
Nor see brief bright November
Rising out of the hills.
You came
When the sun was set and the bough bent
To find the curtness of winter
The completed act.

You may well say, but with little right
"I never trusted autumn"
Who never sought the root
Of sharp October sorrel
And flame red trees
Or knew the wise and final peace
Red-browning autumn brought
To one whom you loved, and left
To face the dark alone.

Suspension

We entered silence
Before the clock struck

Red wine is caught between the crystal
And your fingers
The air solidifys around your mouth.
Once-wind has sucked the curtains in
Like fright, against the evening wall
Prepared for storm   Before the room
Exhales   Your lips unfold.
Within their sudden opening
I hear the clock
Begin to speak again.

I remember now, with the filled crystal
Shattered, the wind-whipped curtains
Bound, and the cold storm
Finally broken,
How the room felt
When your word was spoken—
Warm
As the center of your palms
And as unfree.

CABLES
TO RAGE

(1970)

for Elizabeth and Jonno
my presents

Rites of passage

to MLK jr.

Now rock the boat to a fare-thee-well.
Once we suffered dreaming
Into the place where the children are playing
their child's games
where the children are hoping
knowledge survives if
unknowing
they follow the game
without winning.

Their fathers are dying
back to the freedom of wise children playing
at knowing
their fathers are dying
whose deaths will not free them
of growing from knowledge
of knowing
when the game becomes foolish
a dangerous pleading
for time out of power

Quick
children kiss us
we are growing through dream.

Summer oracle

Without expectation
there is no end
to the shocks of morning
or even a small summer.

Now the image is fire
blackening the vague lines
into defiance across the city.
The image is fire
sun warming us in a cold country
barren of symbols for love.

Now I have forsaken order
and imagine you into fire
untouchable in a magician's coat
covered with signs of destruction and birth
sewn with griffins and arrows and hammers
and gold sixes stitched into your hem
your fingers draw fire
but still the old warlocks shun you
for no gourds ring in your sack
no spells bring forth peace
and I am still fruitless and hungry
this summer
the peaches are flinty and juiceless
and cry sour worms.

The image is fire
flaming over you burning off excess
like the blaze planters start
to burn off bagasse from the canefields
after a harvest.

The image is fire
the high sign that rules our summer
I smell it in the charred breeze blowing over
your body
close
hard
essential
under its cloak of lies.

Song

The wild trees have bought me
and will sell you a wind
in the forest of falsehoods
where your search must not end

for their roots are not wise.
Strip our loving of dream
pay its secrets to thunder
and ransom me home.

Beware oaks in laughter
know hemlock is lying
when she sings of defiance
the sand words she is saying

will sift over and bury
while the pale moons I hate
seduce you in phases
through oceans of light.

And the wild trees shall sell me
for safety from lightning
to the sand that will flay me
for their next evening's planting.

They will fill my limp skin
with wild dreams from their root
and grow from my flesh
new handfuls of hate

till our ransom is wasted
and the morning speaks out
in a thin voice of wisdom
that loves me too late.

Spring people

for Jonno

What anger in my hard-won bones
or heritage of water
makes me reject the april
and fear to walk upon the earth
in spring?

At springtime and evening
I know how we came
like new thunders beating the earth
leaving the taste of rain and sunset
all our hungers before us.
Away from the peace of half-truths
and springtime passing unsaid
we came in the touch of fire
came to the sun
lay with the wild earth
until spent and knowing
we brought forth our young.

Now the insolent aprils bedevil
earthy conceits
to remind us that all else is forfeit
and only our blood-hungry children remember
what face we had
what startling eyes.

Rooming houses are old women

Rooming houses are old women
rocking dark windows into their whens
waiting incomplete circles
rocking
rent office to stoop to
community bathrooms to gas rings
and under-bed boxes of once useful garbage
city issued with a twice-a-month check
the young men next door with their loud midnight parties
and fishy rings left in the bathtub
no longer arouse them
from midnight to mealtime no stops inbetween
light breaking to pass through jumbled up windows
and who was it who married the widow that Buzzie's son messed with?

To Welfare and insult from the slow shuffle
from dayswork to shopping bags heavy with leftovers

Rooming houses
are old women waiting
searching
through their darkening windows
the end or beginning of agony
old women seen through half-ajar doors
hoping
they are not waiting
but being
an entrance to somewhere
unknown and desired
and not new.

Bloodbirth

That which is inside of me screaming
beating about for exit or entry
names the wind, wanting winds' voice
wanting winds' power
it is not my heart
and I am trying to tell this
without art or embellishment
with bits of me flying out in all directions
screams memories old pieces of flesh
struck off like dry bark
from a felled tree, bearing
up or out
holding or bring forth
child or demon
is this birth or exorcism or
the beginning machinery of myself
outlining recalling
my father's business—what I must be
about—my own business
minding.

Shall I split
or be cut down
by a word's complexion or the lack of it
and from what direction
will the opening be made
to show the true face of me
lying exposed and together
my children your children their children
bent on our conjugating business.

After a first book

Paper is neither kind nor cruel
only white in its neutrality
and I have for reality now
the brown bar of my arm
moving in broken rhythms
across this dead place.

All the poems I have ever written
are historical reviews of a now absorbed country
a small judgement
hawking and coughing them up
I have ejected them not unlike children
now my throat is clear
perhaps I shall speak again.

All the poems I have ever written
make a small book
the shedding of my past in patched conceits
moulted like snake skin, a book of leavings
now
I can do anything I wish
I can love them or hate them
use them for comfort or warmth
tissues or decoration
dolls or japanese baskets
blankets or spells;
I can use them for magic
lanterns or music
advice or small council
for napkins or past-times or
disposable diapers
I can make fire from them
or kindling
songs or paper chains

Or fold them all into a paper fan
with which to cool my husband's dinner.

Martha

Martha this is a catalog of days
passing before you looked again.
Someday you will browse and order them
at will, or in your necessities.

I have taken a house at the Jersey shore
this summer. It is not my house.
Today the lightning bugs came.

On the first day you were dead.
With each breath the skin of your face moved
falling in like crumpled muslin.
We scraped together the smashed image of flesh
preparing a memory. No words.
No words.

On the eighth day
you startled the doctors
speaking from your deathplace
to reassure us that you were trying.

Martha these are replacement days
should you ever need them
given for those you once demanded and never found.
May this trip be rewarding;
no one can fault you again Martha
for answering necessity too well
and the gods who honor hard work
will keep this second coming
free from that lack of choice
which hindered your first journey
to this Tarot house.

They said
no hope no dreaming
accept this case of flesh as evidence
of life without fire

and wrapped you in an electric blanket
kept ten degrees below life.
Fetal hands curled inward on the icy sheets
your bed was so cold
the bruises could not appear.

On the second day I knew you were alive
because the grey flesh of your face
suffered.

I love you and cannot feel you less than Martha
I love you and cannot split this shaved head
from Martha's pushy straightness
asking
In a smash of mixed symbols
How long must I wander here
In this final house of my father?

On the Solstice I was in Providence.
You know this town because you visited friends here.
It rained in Providence on the Solstice—
I remember we passed through here twice
on route Six through Providence to the Cape
where we spent our second summer
trying for peace or equity, even.
It always seemed to be raining
by the time we got to Providence.
The Kirschenbaums live in Providence
and Blossom and Barry
and Frances. And Frances.
Martha I am in love again.
Listen, Frances, I said on the Solstice
our summer has started.
Today we are witches and with enough energy
to move mountains back.
Think of Martha.

Back in my hideous city
I saw you today. Your hair has grown
and your armpits are scented
by some careful attendant.

Your *Testing testing testing*
explosive syllables warning me
Of *The mountain has fallen into dung*—
no Martha remember remember Martha—
Warning
Dead flowers will not come to your bed again.
The sun has started south
our season is over.

Today you opened your eyes, giving
a blue-filmed history to your mangled words.
They help me understand
how you are teaching yourself to learn
again.

I need you need me
Ie suis Martha I do not speak french kissing
oh Wow, Black and Black . . . Black and . . . beautiful?
Black and becoming
somebody else maybe Erica maybe who sat
in the fourth row behind us in high school
but I never took French with you Martha
and who is this *Madame Erudite*
who is not me?

I find you today in a womb full of patients
blue-robed in various convalescences.
Your eyes are closed you are propped
Into a wheelchair, cornered,
in a parody of resting.
The bright glue of tragedy plasters all eyes
to a television set in the opposite corner
where a man is dying
step by step
in the american ritual going.
Someone has covered you
for this first public appearance
in a hospital gown, a badge of your next step.
Evocative voices flow from the set
and the horror is thick
in this room full of broken and mending receptions.

But no one has told you what it's all about Martha
someone has shot Robert Kennedy
we are drifting closer to what you predicted
and your darkness is indeed speaking
Robert Kennedy is dying Martha
but not you not you not you
he has a bullet in his brain Martha
surgery was never considered for you
since there was no place to start
and no one intended to run you down on a highway
being driven home at 7.30 on a low summer evening
I gave a reading in Harlem that night
and who shall we try for this shaven head now
in the courts of heart Martha
where his murder is televised over and over
with residuals
they have caught the man who shot Robert Kennedy
who was another one of difficult journeys—
he has a bullet in his brain Martha
and much less of a chance than you.

On the first day of July you warned me again
the threads are broken
you darkened into explosive angers and
refused to open your eyes, humming interference
your thoughts are not over Martha
they are you and their task is
to remember Martha
we can help with the other
the mechanics of blood and bone
and you cut through the pain of my words
to warn me again
testing testing whoever passes
must tear out their hearing aids
for the duration
I hear you explaining Neal
my husband whoever must give me a present
he has to give me
himself where I can find him for
where can he look at himself

in the mirror I am making
or over my bed where the window
is locked into battle with a wall?

Now I sit in New Jersey with lightning bugs and
mosquitoes
typing and thinking of you.
Tonight you started seizures
which they say is a temporary relapse
but this lake is far away Martha
and I sit unquiet in New Jersey
and think of you.
I Ching the Book of Changes
says I am impertinent to ask of you obliquely
but I have no direct question
only need.
When I cast an oracle today
it spoke of the Abyssmal again
which of all the Hexagrams
is very difficult but very promising
in it water finds its own level, flowing
out from the lowest point.
And I cast another also that cautioned
the superior man to seek his strength
only in its own season.
Martha what did we learn from our brief season
when the summer grackles rang in my walls?
one and one is too late now
you journey through darkness alone
leafless I sit far from my present house
and the grackles' voices are dying
we shall love each other here if ever at all.

II
Yes foolish prejudice lies
I hear you Martha
that you would never harm my children
but you have forgotten their names
and that you are Elizabeth's godmother.
And you offer me coral rings, watches

even your body
if I will help you sneak home.

No Martha my blood is not muddy my hands
are not dirty to touch
Martha I do not know your night nurse's name
even though she is black
yes I did live in Brighton Beach once
which is almost Rockaway
one bitter winter
but not with your night nurse Martha
and yes I agree this is one hell
of a summer.

No you cannot walk yet Martha
and no the medicines you are given
to quiet your horrors
have not affected your brain
yes it is very hard to think but
it is getting easier and yes Martha
we have loved each other and yes I hope
we still can
no Martha I do not know if we shall ever
sleep in each other's arms again.

   III
It is the middle of August and you are alive
to discomfort. You have been moved
into a utility room across the hall
from the critical ward because your screaming
disturbs the other patients
your bedside table has been moved also
which means you will be there for a while
a favorite now with the floor nurses
who put up a sign on the utility room door
I'M MARTHA HERE DO NOT FORGET ME
PLEASE KNOCK.

A golden attendant named Sukie
bathes you as you proposition her
she is very pretty and very gentle.
The frontal lobe of the brain governs inhibitions
the damage is after all slight
and they say the screaming will pass.

Your daughter Dorrie promises you
will be as good as new, Mama
who only wants to be *Bad as the old.*

I want some truth good hard truth
a sign of youth
we were all young once we had
a good thing going
now I'm making a plan
for a dead rabbit a rare rabbit.
I am dying goddammit dying am I
Dying?
Death is a word you can say now
pain is mortal
I am dying dying for god's sake won't someone please
get me a doctor PLEASE
your screams beat against our faces as you yell
begging relief from the blank cruelty
of a thousand nurses.
A moment of silence breaks
as you accumulate fresh sorrows
then through your pain-fired face
you slip me a wink

Martha Winked.

Your face straightens into impatience
with the loads of shit you are handed
'You're doing just fine Martha what time is it Martha'
'What did you have for supper tonight Martha'
testing testing whoever passes for Martha
you weary of it.

All the people you must straighten out
pass your bedside in the utility room
bringing you cookies
and hoping
you will be kinder than they were.

Go away Mama and Bubie
for 30 years you made me believe
I was shit you shat out for the asking
but I'm not and you'd better believe it
right now would you kindly
stop rubbing my legs
and GET THE HELL OUT OF HERE.
Next week the Bubie brings Teglach
your old favorite
and will you be kinder Martha
than we were to the shell the cocoon
out of which the you is emerging?

IV
No one you were can come so close
to death without dying
into another Martha.
I await you
as we all await her
fearing her honesty
fearing
we may neither love nor dismiss
Martha with the dross burned away
fearing
condemnation from the essential.

You cannot get closer to death than this Martha
the nearest you've come to living yourself

And what about the children

Now we've made a child.
And the dire predictions
have changed into
wild
grim
speculations.
Still the negatives
are waiting
watching
and the relatives
Keep Right On
Touching . . .
    and how much curl
    is right for a girl?

But if it's said
at some future date
that my son's head
is on straight
he won't care
about his
hair
nor give a damn
whose wife
I am.

The dozens

Nothing says that you must see me in the street
with us so close together at that red light
a blind man would have smelled his grocer—
and nothing says that you must say hello
as we pass in the street,
but we have known each other
too well in the dark
for this
and it hurts me when you do not speak.

But no one you were with was quite so fine
that I won't remember it and
suffer you in turn and
in my own fashion which is certainly
not in the street.
For I can count on my telephone
ringing some evening and you
exploding into my room through the receiver
kissing and licking my ear . . .

I hope you will learn your thing
at least
from some of those spiteful noseless
people who surround you
before the centipede
runs out of worlds
one for each foot.

The woman thing

The hunters are back from beating the winter's face
in search of a challenge or task
in search of food
making fresh tracks for their children's hunger
they do not watch the sun
they cannot wear its heat for a sign
of triumph or freedom
the hunters are treading heavily homeward
through snow that is marked
with their own footprints
emptyhanded, they return
snow-maddened, sustained by their rages.

In the night after food they will seek
young girls for their amusement. Now
the hunters are coming
and the unbaked girls flee from their angers.
All this day I have craved
food for my child's hunger.
Emptyhanded the hunters come shouting
injustices drip from their mouths
like stale snow melted in sunlight.

And the womanthing my mother taught me
bakes off its covering of snow
like a rising blackening sun.

A poem for a poet

I think of a coffin's quiet
when I sit in the world of my car
separate and observing
with the windows closed and washed clean
by the rain. I like to sit there
watching other worlds pass. Yesterday evening
I sat in my car on Sheridan Square
flat and broke and a little bit damp
thinking about money and rain and how
the Village broads with their narrow hips
rolled like drunken shovels down Christopher Street.

Then I saw you unmistakeably
darting out between a police car
and what used to be Jim Atkin's the all-night diner
on the corner of Fourth Street
where we sat making bets the last time I saw you
on how many busts we could count through the plateglass windows
in those last skinny hours before dawn
with our light worded-out but still burning
the earlier evening's promise now dregs in a coffee cup—
and I saw you dash out and turn left at the corner
your beard spiky with rain and refusing
shelter under your chin.

I had thought you were dead Jarrell
struck down by a car at sunset on a North Carolina road
or were you the driver
tricked into a fatal swerve by some twilit shadow
or was that Frank O'hara
or Conrad Kent Rivers
and you the lonesome spook in a Windy City motel
draped in the secrets of your convulsive death
all alone
all poets all loved and dying alone
that final death

less real than those deaths you lived
and for which I forgave you.

I watched you hurry down Fourth Street Jarrell
from the world of my car in the rain
remembering our Spring Festival night
at Women's College in North Carolina
and wasn't that world a coffin retreat
of spring whispers romance and rhetoric
Untouched
by the winds buffeting up from Greensboro
and nobody mentioned the Black Revolution
or Sit-Ins or Freedom Rides or SNCC
or cattle-prods in Jackson, Mississippi—
where I was to find myself how many years later;

You were mistaken that night and I told you
in a letter beginning—Dear Jarrell
if you sit in one place long enough
the whole world can pass you by . . .
you were wrong when you said
I took my living too seriously
meaning you were afraid I might take you too seriously
you shouldn't have worried, because
although I always dug you
too much to put you down
I never took you at all
except as a good piece of my first journey South
except as I take you now
gladly and separate
at a distance and wondering as I have so often
how come
being so cool, you weren't also a little bit
black.

And also why have you returned
to this dying city
and what piece of me is it then
buried down there in North Carolina.

Conversation in crisis

I speak to you as a friend speaks
or a true lover
not out of friendship or love
but for a clear meeting
of self upon self
in sight of our hearth
but without fire.

I cherish your words that ring
like late summer thunders
to sing without octave
and fade, having spoken the season.
But I hear the false heat of this voice
as it dries up the sides of your words
coaxing melodies from your tongue
and this curled music is treason.

Must I die in your fever—
or, as the flames wax, take cover
in your heart's culverts
crouched like a stranger
under the scorched leaves of your other burnt loves
until the storm passes over?

Sowing

It is the sink of the afternoon
the children asleep or weary.
I have finished planting the tomatoes
in this brief sun after four days of rain
now there is brown earth under my fingernails
And sun full on my skin
with my head thick as honey
the tips of my fingers are stinging
from the rich earth
but more so from the lack of your body
I have been to this place before
where blood seething commanded
my fingers fresh from the earth
dream of plowing a furrow
whose name should be you.

Making it

My body arcing across your white place
we mingle color and substance
wanting to mantle your cold
I share my face with you
but love becomes a lie
as we suffer through split masks
seeking the other half-self.

We are hung up
in giving
what we wish to be given
ourselves.

On a night
of the full moon

I

Out of my flesh that hungers
and my mouth that knows
comes the shape I am seeking
for reason.
The curve of your body
fits my waiting hand
your flesh warm as sunlight
your lips quick as young birds
between your thighs the sweet
sharp taste of limes.

Thus I hold you
frank in my heart's eye
in my skin's knowing
as my fingers conceive your flesh
I feel your stomach
curving against me.

Before the moon wanes again
we shall come together.

II

And I would be the moon
spoken over your beckoning flesh
breaking against reservations
beaching thought
my hands at your high tide
over and under inside you
and the passing of hungers
attended, forgotten.

Darkly risen
the moon speaks
my eyes
judging your roundness
delightful.

Fantasy and conversation

Speckled frogs leap from my mouth
to drown in the coffee
between our wisdoms
and decision.

I could smile
and turn these frogs into pearls
speak of love, our making and giving.
And if the spell works
will I break down
or build what is broken
into a new house
shook with confusion
will I strike
before our magic
turns colour?

Dreams bite . . .

I
Dreams bite.
The dreamer and his legends
arm at the edge of purpose.
Waking
I see the people of winter
putting off their masks
to stain the earth
red with blood
while on the outer edges of sleep
the people of sun
are carving their own children
into monuments of war.

II
When I am absolute
at once with the black earth
fire
I make my now
and power is spoken
peace
at rest and
hungry means never
or alone
I shall love again

When I am obsolete.

FROM A LAND
WHERE OTHER
PEOPLE LIVE
(1973)

For Each of You

Be who you are and will be
learn to cherish
that boisterous Black Angel that drives you
up one day and down another
protecting the place where your power rises
running like hot blood
from the same source
as your pain.

When you are hungry
learn to eat
whatever sustains you
until morning
but do not be misled by details
simply because you live them.

Do not let your head deny
your hands
any memory of what passes through them
nor your eyes
nor your heart
everything can be used
except what is wasteful
(you will need
to remember this when you are accused of destruction.)
Even when they are dangerous
examine the heart of those machines you hate
before you discard them
and never mourn the lack of their power
lest you be condemned
to relive them.
If you do not learn to hate
you will never be lonely
enough
to love easily
nor will you always be brave
although it does not grow any easier

Do not pretend to convenient beliefs
even when they are righteous
you will never be able to defend your city
while shouting.

Remember our sun
is not the most noteworthy star
only the nearest.

Respect whatever pain you bring back
from your dreaming
but do not look for new gods
in the sea
nor in any part of a rainbow
Each time you love
love as deeply
as if it were
forever
only nothing is
eternal.

Speak proudly to your children
where ever you may find them
tell them
you are the offspring of slaves
and your mother was
a princess
in darkness.

The Day They
Eulogized Mahalia

The day they eulogized Mahalia
the echoes of her big voice were stilled
and the mourners found her
singing out from their sisters mouths
from their mothers toughness
from the funky dust in the corners
of sunday church pews
sweet and dry and simple
and that hated sunday morning fussed over feeling
the songs
singing out from their mothers toughness
would never threaten the lord's retribution
any more.

Now she was safe
acceptable
that big Mahalia
Chicago turned all out
to show her that they cared
but her eyes were closed
And although Mahalia loved our music
nobody sang her favorite song
and while we talked about
what a hard life she had known
and wasn't it too bad Sister Mahalia
didn't have it easier
earlier
Six Black children
burned to death in a day care center
on the South Side
kept in a condemned house
for lack of funds
firemen found their bodies

like huddled lumps of charcoal
with silent mouths and eyes wide open.
Small and without song
six black children found a voice in flame
the day the city eulogized Mahalia.

Equinox

My daughter marks the day that spring begins.
I cannot celebrate spring without remembering
how the bodies of unborn children
bake in their mothers flesh like ovens
consecrated to the flame that eats them
lit by mobiloil and easternstandard
Unborn children in their blasted mothers
floating like small monuments
in an ocean of oil.

The year my daughter was born
DuBois died in Accra while I
marched into Washington
to a death knell of dreaming
which 250,000 others mistook for a hope
believing only Birmingham's black children
were being pounded into mortar in churches
that year
some of us still thought
Vietnam was a suburb of Korea.

Then John Kennedy fell off the roof
of Southeast Asia
and shortly afterward my whole house burned down
with nobody in it
and on the following sunday my borrowed radio announced
that Malcolm was shot dead
and I ran to reread
all that he had written
because death was becoming such an excellent measure
of prophecy
As I read his words the dark mangled children
came streaming out of the atlas
Hanoi Angola Guinea-Bissau Mozambique Pnam-Phen
merged into Bedford-Stuyvesant and Hazelhurst Mississippi
haunting my New York tenement that terribly bright
    summer

while Detroit and Watts and San Francisco were burning
I lay awake in stifling Broadway nights afraid
for whoever was growing in my belly
and suppose it started earlier than planned
who would I trust to take care that my daughter
did not eat poisoned roaches
when I was gone?

If she did, it doesn't matter
because I never knew it.
Today both children came home from school
talking about spring and peace
and I wonder if they will ever know it
I want to tell them we have no right to spring
because our sisters and brothers are burning
because every year the oil grows thicker
and even the earth is crying
because black is beautiful but currently
going out of style
that we must be very strong
and love each other
in order to go on living.

Progress Report

These days
when you do say hello I am never sure
if you are being saucy or experimental or
merely protecting some new position.
Sometimes you gurgle while asleep
and I know tender places still intrigue you.
Now
when you question me on love
shall I recommend a dictionary
or myself?

You are the child of wind and ravens I created
always my daughter
I cannot recognize
the currents where you swim and dart
through my loving
upstream to your final place of birth
but you never tire of hearing
how I crept out of my mother's house
at dawn, with an olive suitcase
crammed with books and fraudulent letters
and an unplayed guitar.

Sometimes I see myself flash through your eyes
in a moment
caught between history and obedience
that moment grows each day
before you comply
as, when did washing dishes
change from privilege to chore?
I watch the hollows deepen above your hips
and wonder if I have taught you Black enough
until I see
all kinds of loving still intrigue you
as you grow more and more
dark
rude and tender
and unfraid.

What you took for granted once
you now refuse to take at all
even I
knock before I enter
the shoals of furious choices
not my own
that flood through your secret reading
nightly, under cover.
I have not yet seen you, but
I hear the pages rustle
from behind closed doors.

Good Mirrors
Are Not Cheap

It is a waste of time hating a mirror
or its reflection
instead of stopping the hand
that makes glass with distortions
slight enough to pass
unnoticed
until one day you peer
into your face
under a merciless white light
and the fault in a mirror slaps back
becoming
what you think
is the shape of your error
and if I am beside that self
you destroy me
or if you can see
the mirror is lying
you shatter the glass
choosing another blindness
and slashed helpless hands.

Because at the same time
down the street
a glassmaker is grinning
turning out new mirrors that lie
selling us
new clowns
at cut rate.

Black Mother Woman

I cannot recall you gentle
yet through your heavy love
I have become
an image of your once delicate flesh
split with deceitful longings.

When strangers come and compliment me
your aged spirit takes a bow
jingling with pride
but once you hid that secret
in the center of furies
hanging me
with deep breasts and wiry hair
with your own split flesh
and long suffering eyes
buried in myths of little worth.

But I have peeled away your anger
down to the core of love
and look mother
I Am
a dark temple where your true spirit rises
beautiful
and tough as chestnut
stanchion against your nightmare of weakness
and if my eyes conceal
a squadron of conflicting rebellions
I learned from you
to define myself
through your denials.

As I Grow Up Again

A little boy wears my mistakes
like a favorite pair of shorts
outgrown
at six
my favorite excuse was morning
and I remember that I hated
springs change.

At play within my childhood
my son works hard
learning
the doors that do not open easily
and which clocks will not work
he toys with anger like a young cat
testing its edges
slashing through the discarded box
where I laid my childish dreams to rest
and brought him brown and wriggling
to his own house.

He learns there through my error
winning with secrets
I do not need to know.

The
Seventh Sense

Women
who build nations
learn
to love
men
who build nations
learn
to love
children
building sand castles
by the rising sea.

New Year's Day

The day feels put together hastily
like a gift for grateful beggars
being better than no time at all
but the bells are ringing
in cities I have never visited
and my name is printed over doorways
I have never seen
While extracting a bone
or whatever is tender or fruitful
from the core of indifferent days
I have forgotten
the touch of sun
cutting through uncommitted mornings
The night is full of messages
I cannot read
I am too busy forgetting
air like fur on my tongue
and these tears
which do not come from sadness
but from grit in a sometimes wind

Rain falls like tar on my skin
my son picks up a chicken heart at dinner
asking
does this thing love?
Deft unmalicious fingers of ghosts
pluck over my dreaming
hiding whatever it is of sorrow
that would profit me

I am deliberate
and afraid
of nothing.

Teacher

I make my children promises in wintry afternoons
like lunchtime stories
when my feet hurt from talking too much
and not enough movement except in my own
worn down at the heel shoes
except in the little circle of broken down light
I am trapped in
the intensities of my own (our) situation
where what we need and do not have
deadens us
and promises sound like destruction
white snowflakes clog the passages
drifting through the halls and corridors
while I tell stories with no ending
at lunchtime
the children's faces bear uneasy smiles
like a heavy question
I provide food with a frightening efficiency
the talk is free/dom meaning state
condition of being
We are elementary forces colliding in free fall.

And who will say I made promises
better kept in confusion
than time
grown tall and straight in a season of snow
in a harsh time of the sun that withers
who will say as they build
ice castles at noon
living the promises I made
these children
who will say
look—we have laid out the new cities
with more love than our dreams
Who will hear
freedom's bell deaden
in the clang of the gates of the prisons

where snow-men melt into darkness
unforgiven and so remembered
while the hot noon speaks in a fiery voice?

How we romped through so many winters
made snowballs play at war
rubbing snow against our brown faces
and they tingled and grew bright
in the winter sun
instead of chocolate we rolled snow
over our tongues
until it melted like sugar
burning the cracks in our lips
and we shook our numbed fingers
all the way home
remembering
summer was coming.

As the promises I make children
sprout like wheat from early spring's wager
who will hear freedom
ring in the chains of promise
who will forget the curse
of the outsider
who will not recognize our season
as free
who will say
Promise corrupts
what it does not invent.

Moving Out or
The End of Cooperative Living

I am so glad to be moving
away from this prison for black and white faces
assaulting each other with our joint oppression
competing for who pays the highest price for this privilege
I am so glad I am moving
technicoloured complaints aimed at my head
mash themselves on my door like mosquitoes
sweep like empty ladles through the lobby of my eyes
each time my lips move sideways
the smile shatters
on the in thing that races
dictator through our hallways
on concrete faces on soul compactors
on the rhetoric of incinerators and plastic drapes
for the boiler room
on legends of broken elevators
blowing my morning cool
avoiding me in the corridors
dropping their load on my face down 24 stories
of lives in a spectrumed madhouse
pavillion of gnats and nightmare remembering
once we all saved like beggars
to buy our way into this castle
of fantasy and forever now
I am so glad to be moving.

Last month a tenant was asked to leave
because someone saw him
wandering one morning up and down the tenth floor
with no clothes on
having locked himself out the night before
with the garbage
he could not fit into the incinerator
but it made no difference
the floor captain cut the leads to his cable TV
and he left covered in tangled wires of shame

his apartment was reconsecrated by a fumigator
I am so glad I am moving

Although workmen will descend at $100 an hour
to scrape my breath from the walls
to refinish the air and the floors with their eyes
and charge me with the exact amount
of whatever I have coming back to me
called equity
I am so glad to be moving
from the noise of psychic footsteps
beating a tune that is not my own
louder than any other sound in the neighborhood
except the blasting that goes on all day and all night
from the city's new toilet being built
outside the main entrance
from the spirits who live in the locks
of the other seven doors
bellowing secrets of living hells revealed
but not shared
for everybody's midnights know what the walls hide
our toilets are made of glass
wired for sound

24 stories
full of tears flushing at midnight
our only community room
children set their clocks to listen at the tissue walls
gazing upward from their stools
from one flight to another
catching the neighbors in private struggles
next morning it will all be discussed
at length in the elevators
with no secrets left
I am so glad to be moving
no more coming home at night to dream
of caged puppies
grinding their teeth into cartoonlike faces
that half plead and half snicker

then fold under and vanish
back into snarling strangers
I am so glad I am moving.

But when this grim house goes
slipping into the sewer prepared for it
then this whole city can read
its own obituary
written on the broken record of dreams
of ordinary people
who wanted what they could not get
and so pretended to be someone else
ordinary people having
what they never learned to want
themselves
and so becoming
pretension concretized.

Moving In

"It is the worst of luck to bring into a new house from the old bread salt or broomstick."

Salt Bread and Broom
be still.
I leave you guardian
against gone places
I have loved
your loss
in a green promise
making new
Salt
Bread
and Broom
remove me from the was
I still am
to now
becoming
here this house
forever blessed.

Neighbors

For D. D.

We made strong poems for each other
exchanging formulas for our own particular magic
all the time pretending
we were not really witches
and each time we would miss
some small ingredient
that one last detail
that would make the spell work
Each one of us
too busy
hearing our other voices
the sound of our own guards
calling the watch at midnight
assuring us
we were still safely asleep
so when it came time to practice
what we had learned
one grain was always missing
one word unsaid
so the pot did not boil
the sweet milk would curdle
or the bright wound went on bleeding
and each of us would go back
to her own particular magic
confirmed
believing
she was always alone
believing
the other was always
lying
in wait.

Change of Season

Am I to be cursed forever with becoming
somebody else on the way to myself?

Walking backward I fall
into summers behind me
salt with wanting
lovers or friends a job wider shoes
a cool drink
freshness something to bite into
a place to hide out of the rain
out of the shifting melange of seasons
where the cruel boys I chased
and their skinny dodgeball sisters
flamed and died in becoming
the brown autumn
left in search of who tore the streamers down
at graduation christmas my wedding day
and as winter wore out the babies came
angry effort and reward
in their appointed seasons
my babies tore out of me
like poems
after
I slept and woke to the thought
that promise had come again
this time more sure than the dream of being
sweet sixteen and somebody else
walking five miles through the august city
with a free dog
thinking
now we will be the allamerican family
we had just gotten a telephone
and the next day my sister cut his leash on Broadway
that dog of my childhood bays at the new moon
as I reach into time up to my elbows
extracting the taste and sharp smell
of my first lover's neck

rough as the skin of a brown pear ripening
I was terribly sure I would come forever to april
with my first love who died on a sunday morning
poisoned and wondering
would summer ever come.

As I face an ocean of seasons they start
to separate into distinct and particular faces
listening to the cover beginning to crack open
and whether or not the fruit is worth waiting
thistles and arrows and apples are blooming
the individual beautiful faces are smiling and moving
even the pavement begins to flow into new concretions
the eighth day is coming

I have paid dearly in time for love I hoarded
unseen
summer goes into my words
and comes out reason.

Generation II

A Black girl
going
into the woman
her mother
desired
and prayed for
walks alone
and afraid
of both
their angers.

Love, Maybe

Always
in the middle
of our bloodiest battles
you lay down your arms
like flowering mines

to conqueror me home.

Relevant Is Different
Points on the Circle
to BWC

History
bless me with my children's growing rebellion
with love in another tongue
teach me what my pride will not savor
like the fabled memory of elephants
I have loved them and watched over them
as the bird forgets but the trap doesn't
and I shall be buried with the bones of an eagle
with a fierce detachment
and legends of the slain buffalo.

This is a country where other people live

When agate replaces dead wood
slowly the opal and bone become one.
A phoenix named Angela
nests in my children's brain
already
the growing herds of bison unnoticed
are being hunted down the federal canyons
of Yellowstone Park.

Signs

No one is left here to eat by my fire.
My children have gone to the wood
with their earth coloured laughter
stitched up in a market blanket
I wore to announce my coming of age and that day
the other girls went pale and wanting
in the noon sun.

Let their journey be free from ghosts.
I have heard the old spirits chatter
planning my downfall
for my yams have always been eaten with pleasure
and my body has not been unfruitful
I do not squander my days at the market
nor bargain for what I cannot sell
I do not cover my yams with a cloth
when creditors pass
pretending they belong to another.
But I have only two children.
Neither was born by conjure nor in hiding
now they go to the wood
to the night to the gradual breaking
and they will return
men and silent
draped in impatience and indigo
signs of our separation.

As I go to wash myself before sun
I search my door-yard and wonder
if I will find the shattered pot
left as a sign to warn me
they shall never return.

Conclusion

Passing men in the street who are dead
becomes a common occurrence
but loving one of them
is no solution.
I believe in love as I believe in our children
but I was born Black and without illusions
and my vision
which differs from yours
is clear
although sometimes restricted.

I have watched you at midnight
moving through casual sleep
wishing I could afford the non-desperate dreams
that stir you
to wither and fade into partial solutions.
Your nights are wintery long and very young
full of symbols of purity and forgiveness
and a meek jesus that rides through your cities
on a barren ass whose braying
does not include a future tense.
But I wear my nights as I wear my life
and my dying
absolute and unforgiven
nuggets of compromise and decision
fossilized by fierce midsummer sun
and when I dream
I move through a Black land
where the future
glows eternal and green
but where the symbols for now
are bloody and unrelenting
rooms
where confused children

with wooden stumps for fingers
play at war
who cannot pick up their marbles
and run away home
whenever nightmare threatens.

A Song of
Names and Faces

I walk across noon with you today
knowing you for a mistake in my blood
calling you with yesterday's voice
and you are wise to forget the rules
of yesterday's game. But creepers tickle
our elbows as we circle the park
and tomorrow
the little red gourds hung on the cusp
of the moon of cherries blackening
will rattle a winter's song.

I cannot record the face you wear
in this afternoon
because I have not judged myself.
We shall walk as far as we can
until we tire
hoping
there will be someone
to amuse each of us
on the way back home.

I always forget how the year began
by the time midsummer comes on me.

We first met at noontime
during the moon of snowblindness
Shall I call you today's name tomorrow
or forget you exist at all?

Movement Song

I have studied the tight curls on the back of your neck
moving away from me
beyond anger or failure
your face in the evening schools of longing
through mornings of wish and ripen
we were always saying goodbye
in the blood in the bone over coffee
before dashing for elevators going
in opposite directions
without goodbyes.

Do not remember me as a bridge nor a roof
as the maker of legends
nor as a trap
door to that world
where black and white clericals
hang on the edge of beauty in five oclock elevators
twitching their shoulders to avoid other flesh
and now
there is someone to speak for them
moving away from me into tomorrows
morning of wish and ripen
your goodbye is a promise of lightning
in the last angels hand
unwelcome and warning
the sands have run out against us
we were rewarded by journeys
away from each other
into desire
into mornings alone
where excuse and endurance mingle
conceiving decision.
Do not remember me
as disaster
nor as the keeper of secrets

I am a fellow rider in the cattle cars
watching
you move slowly out of my bed
saying we cannot waste time
only ourselves.

The Winds
of Orisha

I

This land will not always be foreign.
How many of its women ache to bear their stories
robust and screaming like the earth erupting grain
or thrash in padded chains mute as bottles
hands fluttering traces of resistance
on the backs of once lovers
half the truth
knocking in the brain like an angry steampipe
how many
long to work or split open
so bodies venting into silence
can plan the next move?

Tiresias took 500 years they say to progress into woman
growing smaller and darker and more powerful
until nut-like, she went to sleep in a bottle
Tiresias took 500 years to grow into woman
so do not despair of your sons.

II

Impatient legends speak through my flesh
changing this earths formation
spreading
I will become myself
an incantation
dark raucous many-shaped characters
leaping back and forth across bland pages
and Mother Yemonja raises her breasts to begin my labour
near water
the beautiful Oshun and I lie down together
in the heat of her body truth my voice comes stronger
Shango will be my brother roaring out of the sea
earth shakes our darkness swelling into each other
warning winds will announce us living

as Oya, Oya my sister my daughter
destroys the crust of the tidy beaches
and Eshu's black laughter turns up the neat sleeping sand.

III
The heart of this country's tradition is its wheat men
dying for money
dying for water for markets for power
over all people's children
they sit in their chains on their dry earth
before nightfall
telling tales as they wait for their time
of completion
hoping the young ones can hear them
earth-shaking fears wreath their blank weary faces
most of them have spent their lives and their wives
in labour
most of them have never seen beaches
but as Oya my sister moves out of the mouths
of their sons and daughters against them
I will swell up from the pages of their daily heralds
leaping out of the almanacs
instead of an answer to their search for rain
    they will read me
the dark cloud
meaning something entire
and different.

When the winds of Orisha blow
even the roots of grass
quicken.

Who Said
It Was Simple

There are so many roots to the tree of anger
that sometimes the branches shatter
before they bear.

Sitting in Nedicks
the women rally before they march
discussing the problematic girls
they hire to make them free.
An almost white counterman passes
a waiting brother to serve them first
and the ladies neither notice nor reject
the slighter pleasures of their slavery.
But I who am bound by my mirror
as well as my bed
see causes in colour
as well as sex

and sit here wondering
which me will survive
all these liberations.

Dear Toni Instead of a Letter of Congratulation Upon Your Book and Your Daughter Whom You Say You Are Raising To Be a Correct Little Sister

I can see your daughter walking down streets of love
in revelation;
but raising her up to be a correct little sister
is doing your mama's job all over again.
And who did you make on the edge of Harlem's winter
hard and black
while the inside was undetermined
swirls of color and need
shifting, remembering
were you making another self to rediscover
in a new house and a new name
in a new place next to a river of blood
or were you putting the past together
pooling everything learned
into a new and continuous woman
divorced
from the old shit we share
and shared and sharing need not share again?

I see your square delicate jawbone
the mark of a Taurus (or Leo) as well as the ease
with which you deal with your pretensions.
I dig your going and becoming
the lessons you teach your daughter
our history
for I am your sister corrected and
already raised up
our daughters will explore the old countries
as curious visitors to our season
using their own myths to keep themselves sharp.
I have known you over and over again
as I've lived throughout this city
taking it in storm and morning strolls

through Astor Place and under the Canal Street Bridge
The Washington Arch like a stone raised to despair
and Riverside Drive too close to the dangerous predawn
waters and 129th Street between Lenox and Seventh
burning my blood but not black enough
and threatening to become home.

I first saw you behind a caseworker's notebook
defying upper Madison Avenue and my roommate's concern
the ghost of Maine lobsterpots trailing behind you
and I followed you into east fourth street and out
through Bellevue's side entrance one night
into the respectable vineyards of Yeshivas intellectual gloom
and there I lost you between the books and the games
until I rose again out of Jackson Mississippi
to find you in an office down the hall from mine
calmly studying term papers like maps
marking off stations
on our trip through the heights of Convent Avenue
teaching english our children citycollege
softer and tougher and more direct
and putting your feet up on a desk you say Hi
I'm going to have a baby so now I can really indulge myself.
Through that slim appraisal of your world
I felt you
grinning and plucky and a little bit scared
perhaps of the madness past that had relieved you
through your brittle young will of iron
into the fire of whip steel.

I have a daughter also
who does not remind me of you
but she too has deep aquatic eyes that are burning and curious.
As she moves through taboos
whirling myths like gay hoops over her head
I know beyond fear and history
that our teaching means keeping trust
with less and less correctness
only with ourselves—
History may alter

old pretenses and victories
but not the pain my sister never the pain.

In my daughter's name
I bless your child with the mother she has
with a future of warriors and growing fire.
But with tenderness also,
for we are landscapes, Toni,
printed upon them as surely
as water etches feather on stone.
Our girls will grow into their own
Black Women
finding their own contradictions
that they will come to love
as I love you.

[September 1971]

Prologue

Haunted by poems beginning with I
seek out those whom I love who are deaf
to whatever does not destroy
or curse the old ways that did not serve us
while history falters and our poets are dying
choked into silence by icy distinction
their death rattles blind curses
and I hear even my own voice becoming
a pale strident whisper
At night sleep locks me into an echoless coffin
sometimes at noon I dream
there is nothing to fear
now standing up in the light of my father sun
without shadow
I speak without concern for the accusations
that I am too much or too little woman
that I am too black or too white
or too much myself
and through my lips come the voices
of the ghosts of our ancestors
living and moving among us
Hear my heart's voice as it darkens
pulling old rhythms out of the earth
that will receive this piece of me
and a piece of each one of you
when our part in history quickens again
and is over:

Hear
the old ways are going away
and coming back pretending change
masked as denunciation and lament
masked as a choice
between eager mirrors that blur and distort
us in easy definitions
until our image
shatters along its fault

while the other half of that choice
speaks to our hidden fears with a promise
that our eyes need not seek any truer shape—
a face at high noon particular and unadorned—
for we have learned to fear
the light from clear water might destroy us
with reflected emptiness or a face without tongue
with no love or with terrible penalties
for any difference
and even as I speak remembered pain is moving
shadows over my face, my own voice fades and
my brothers and sisters are leaving;

Yet when I was a child
whatever my mother thought would mean survival
made her try to beat me whiter every day
and even now the colour of her bleached ambition
still forks throughout my words
but I survived
and didn't I survive confirmed
to teach my children where her errors lay
etched across their faces between the kisses
that she pinned me with asleep
and my mother beating me
as white as snow melts in the sunlight
loving me into her bloods black bone—

the home of all her secret hopes and fears
and my dead father whose great hands
weakened in my judgement
whose image broke inside of me
beneath the weight of failure
helps me to know who I am not
weak or mistaken
my father loved me alive
to grow and hate him
and now his grave voice joins hers
within my words rising and falling
are my sisters and brothers listening?

The children remain
like blades of grass over the earth and
all the children are singing
louder than mourning
all their different voices sound like a raucous question
but they do not fear the blank and empty mirrors
they have seen their faces defined in a hydrants puddle
before the rainbows of oil obscured them.
The time of lamentation and curses is passing.

My mother survives now
through more than chance or token.
Although she will read what I write with embarrassment
or anger
and a small understanding
my children do not need to relive my past
in strength nor in confusion
nor care that their holy fires
may destroy
more than my failures

Somewhere in the landscape past noon
I shall leave a dark print
of the me that I am
and who I am not
etched in a shadow of angry and remembered loving
and their ghosts will move
whispering through them
with me none the wiser
for they will have buried me
either in shame
or in peace.

And the grasses will still be
Singing.

[November 1971]

New York
Head Shop and
Museum

(1974)

TO THE CHOCOLATE PEOPLE
OF AMERICA

Chocolate people don't melt in water
they melt in your eyes.
Jonathan Rollins—1971

New York City 1970

How do you spell change like frayed slogan underwear
with the emptied can of yesterdays' meanings
with yesterdays' names?
And what does the we-bird see with
who has lost its I's?

There is nothing beautiful left in the streets of this city.
I have come to believe in death and renewal by fire.
Past questioning the necessities of blood
or why it must be mine or my children's time
that will see the grim city quake to be reborn perhaps
blackened again but this time with a sense of purpose;
tired of the past tense forever, of assertion and repetition
of the ego-trips through an incomplete self
where two years ago proud rang for promise but now
it is time for fruit and all the agonies are barren—
only the children are growing:

For how else can the self become whole
save by making self into its own new religion?
I am bound like an old lover—a true believer—
to this city's death by accretion and slow ritual,
and I submit to its penance for a trial
as new steel is tried
I submit my children also to its death throes and agony
and they are not even the city's past lovers. But I submit them
to the harshness and growing cold to the brutalizations
which if survived
will teach them strength or an understanding of how strength is gotten
and will not be forgotten: It will be their city then:
I submit them
loving them above all others save myself
to the fire to the rage to the ritual scarifications
to be tried as new steel is tried;
and in its wasting the city shall try them
as the blood-splash of a royal victim
tries the hand of the destroyer.

II

I hide behind tenements and subways in fluorescent alleys
watching as flames walk the streets of an empire's altar
raging through the veins of the sacrificial stenchpot
smeared upon the east shore of a continent's insanity
conceived in the psychic twilight of murderers and pilgrims
rank with money and nightmare and too many useless people
who will not move over nor die, who cannot bend
even before the winds of their own preservation
even under the weight of their own hates
Who cannot amend nor conceive nor even learn to share
their own visions
who bomb my children into mortar in churches
and work plastic offal and metal and the flesh of their enemies
into subway rush-hour temples where obscene priests
finger and worship each other in secret
and think they are praying when they squat
to shit money-pebbles shaped like their parents' brains—
who exist to go into dust to exist again
grosser and more swollen and without ever relinquishing
space or breath or energy from their private hoard.

I do not need to make war nor peace
with these prancing and murderous deacons
who refuse to recognize their role in this covenant we live upon
and so have come to fear and despise even their own children;
but I condemn myself, and my loves
past and present
and the blessed enthusiasms of all my children
to this city
without reason or future
without hope
to be tried as the new steel is tried
before trusted to slaughter.

I walk down the withering limbs of my last discarded house
and there is nothing worth salvage left in this city
but the faint reedy voices like echoes
of once beautiful children.

To My Daughter The Junkie
On A Train

Children we have not borne
bedevil us by becoming
themselves
painfully sharp and unavoidable
like a needle in our flesh.

Coming home on the subway from a PTA meeting
of minds committed like murder
or suicide
to their own private struggle
a long-legged girl with a horse in her brain
slumps down beside me
begging to be ridden asleep
for the price of a midnight train
free from desire.
Little girl on the nod
if we are measured by the dreams we avoid
then you are the nightmare
of all sleeping mothers
rocking back and forth
the dead weight of your arms
locked about our necks
heavier than our habit
of looking for reasons.

My corrupt concern will not replace
what you once needed
but I am locked into my own addictions
and offer you my help, one eye
out
for my own station.
Roused and deprived
your costly dream explodes
into a terrible technicoloured laughter

at my failure
up and down across the aisle
women avert their eyes
as the other mothers who became useless
curse their children who became junk.

To Desi As Joe As Smoky
The Lover of 115th Street

Who are you
that your name comes
broken by the speeding cars along the East Side Drive
tumbling out of the concrete wall flowers
as I pass
Desi as Joe as Smoky the Lover of 115th Street?

There was nothing furtive about the swirls
of neon-bright magenta
prancing off your fingertips
like ideal selves
is the dream you
valued more
because you glanced over your shoulder
as you wrote
the first letter
undecided
its flourish
shaped like a question mark?

But there was nothing at all
to see over your shoulder
except my eyes in a passing tide of cars
wondering
if you wrote under a culvert
so the approaching storm around us
would not wash you away.

There was nothing at all
furtive
about your magenta scrawling
but I saw the bright sweat
running off your childhood's face
as you glanced behind you
choosing that wall beneath a bridge
where so many others had written

before
that the colours merged into
one sunlit mosaic
face without name
decorating a highway
on the very edge of Manhattan.

The American Cancer Society Or
There Is More Than One Way
To Skin A Coon

Of all the ways in which this country
Prints its death upon me
Selling me cigarettes is one of the most certain.
Yet every day I watch my son digging
ConEdison GeneralMotors GarbageDisposal
Out of his nose as he watches a 3 second spot
On How To Stop Smoking
And it makes me sick to my stomach.
For it is not by cigarettes
That you intend to destroy my children.

Not even by the cold white light of moon-walks
While half the boys I knew
Are doomed to quicker trips by a different capsule;
No, the american cancer destroys
By seductive and reluctant admission
For instance
Black women no longer give birth through their ears
And therefore must have A Monthly Need For Iron:
For instance
Our Pearly teeth are *not* racially insured
And therefore must be Gleemed For Fewer Cavities:
For instance
Even though all astronauts are white
Perhaps Black People *can* develop
Some of those human attributes
Requiring
Dried dog food frozen coffee instant oatmeal
Depilatories deodorants detergents
And other assorted plastic.

And this is the surest sign I know
That the american cancer society is dying—
It has started to dump its symbols onto Black People
Convincing proof that those symbols are now useless
And far more lethal than emphysema.

A Sewerplant Grows In Harlem
Or
I'm A Stranger Here Myself
When Does The Next Swan Leave

How is the word made flesh made steel made shit
by ramming it into No Exit like a homemade bomb
until it explodes
smearing itself
made real
against our already filthy windows
or by flushing it out in a verbal fountain?
Meanwhile the editorial They—
who are no less powerful—
prepare to smother the actual Us
with a processed flow of all our shit
non-verbal.

Have you ever risen in the night
bursting with knowledge and the world
dissolves toward any listening ear
into which you can pour
whatever it was you knew
before waking
Only to find all ears asleep
or drugged perhaps by a dream of words
because as you scream into them over and over
nothing stirs
and the mind you have reached is not a working mind
please hang up and die again? The mind
you have reached is not a working mind
Please hang up
And die again.

Talking to some people is like talking to a toilet.

A Birthday Memorial To Seventh Street

I

I tarry in days shaped like the high staired street
where I became a woman
between two funeral parlors next door to each other
sharing a dwarf
who kept watch for the hearses
Fox's Bar on the corner
playing happy birthday to a boogie beat
Old slavic men cough in the spring thaw
hawking
painted candles cupcakes fresh eggs
from under their dull green knitted caps
when the right winds blow
the smell of bird seed and malt
from the breweries across the river
stops even our worst hungers.

One crosstown bus each year
carries silence into overcrowded hallways
plucking madmen out of the mailboxes
from under stairwells
from cavorting over rooftops in the full moon
cutting short the mournful songs that used to soothe me
before they would cascade to laughter every afternoon
at four PM
behind a door that never opened
Then masked men in white coats dismount
to take the names of anyone
who has not paid the rent in three months
they peel off layers of christmas seals
and batter down the doors into bare apartments
where they duly note the shape of each obscenity
upon the wall
and hunt those tenants down
to make new vacancies.

II

These were some of my lovers who were processed
through the corridors of Bellevue Mattewean Brooklyn State
the Women's House of D. St. Vincent's and the Tombs
to be stapled on tickets for a one way ride
on the unmarked train that travels
once a year
across the country east to west
filled with New York's rejected lovers
ones who played with all their stakes
who could not win nor learn to lie—
we were much fewer then—
who failed the entry tasks of Seventh Street
and were returned back home
to towns with names like Oblong and Vienna
(called Vyanna)
Cairo Sesser Cave-In-Rock and Legend.
Once a year the train stops unannounced
at midnight
just outside of town
returning the brave of Bonegap and Tuskegee
of Pawnee Falls and Rabbittown
of Anazine and Elegant and Intercourse
leaving them beyond the edge of town
like dried up bones sucked clean of marrow
but rattling with city-like hardness
the soft wood
petrified to stone in Seventh Street.
The train screams
warning the town of coming trouble
then moves on.

III

I walk over Seventh Street
stone at midnight
two years away from forty
and the ghosts of old friends

precede me down the street in welcome
bopping in and out of doorways
with a boogie beat
Freddie sails before me like a made-up bat
his Zorro cape just level with the stoops
he pirouettes over the garbage cans
a bundle of drugged delusions
hanging from his belt
while Joan with a hand across her throat
sings
unafraid of silence anymore
and Marion who lived on the scraps of breath
left in the refuse of strangers
searches the gutter with her nightmare eyes
tripping over the brown girl
young in her eyes and fortune
nimble as birch
and I try to recall her name
as Clement comes
smiling from a distance
his finger raised in counsel
or in blessing
over us all.

Seventh Street swells into midnight
memory ripe as a bursting grape
my head is a museum
full of other people's eyes
like stones in a dark churchyard
where I kneel praying
that my children
will not die politely
either.

One Year To Life On The Grand Central Shuttle

If we hate the rush hour subways
who ride them every day
why hasn't there been a New York City Subway Riot
some bloody rush-hour revolution
where a snarl
goes on from push to a shove
that does not stop
at the platform's edge
the whining of automated trains
will drown out the screams
of our bloody and releasing testament
to a last chance or hope of change.

But hope is counter-revolutionary.
Pressure cooks
but we have not exploded
flowing in and out instead each day
like a half-digested mass
for a final stake impales our dreams
and watering down each trip's fury
is the someday foolish hope
that at the next stop
some door will open for us
to fresh air and light and home.

When we realize how
much of us is spent
in rush hour subways
underground
no real exit
it will matter less
what token we pay
for change.

The Workers Rose On May Day
Or
Postscript To Karl Marx

Down Wall Street
the students marched for peace
Above, construction workers looking on remembered
how it was for them in the old days
before their closed shop white security
and daddy pays the bills
so they climbed down the girders
and taught their sons a lesson
called Marx is a victim of the generation gap
called I grew up the hard way so will you
called
the limits of a sentimental vision.

When the passion play was over
and the dust had cleared on Wall Street
500 Union workers together with police
had mopped up Foley Square
with 2000 of their striking sons
who broke and ran
before their fathers chains.

Look here Karl Marx
the apocalyptic vision of amerika!
Workers rise and win
and have not lost their chains
but swing them
side by side with the billyclubs in blue
securing Wall Street
against the striking students.

Cables to Rage
or
I've Been Talking on This Street
Corner a Hell of a Long Time

This is how I came to be loved
by loving myself loveless.

One day I slipped in the snowy gutter of Brighton Beach
and the booted feet passing
me by on the curb squished my laundry ticket
into the slush and I thought oh fuck it now
I'll never get my clean sheet and I cried bitter tears
into the snow under my cheek in that gutter in Brighton Beach
Brooklyn where I was living because it was cheap

In a furnished room with cooking privileges
and there was an old thrown-away mama who lived down the
     hall
a yente who sat all day long in our common kitchen
weeping because her children made her live with a schwartze
and while she wept she drank up all my Cream Soda
every day before I came home.
Then she sat and watched me watching my chicken feet stewing
on the Fridays when I got paid
and she taught me to boil old corn in the husk
to make it taste green and fresh.
There were not many pleasures in that winter
and I loved Cream Soda
there were not many people in that winter
and I came to hate that old woman.
The winter I got fat on stale corn on the cob
and chicken foot stew and the day before Christmas
having no presents to wrap
I poured two ounces of Nux Vomica into a bottle of Cream Soda
and listened to the old lady puke all night long.

When spring came I crossed the river again
moving up in the world six and half stories
and one day on the corner of eighth street across from Wanamakers
which had burned down while I was away in Brooklyn—
where I caught the bus for work every day
a bus driver slowed down at the bus stop one morning—
I was late it was raining and my jacket was soaked—
and then speeded past without stopping when he saw my face.

I have been given other doses of truth—
that particular form of annihilation—
shot through by the cold eye of the way things are baby
and left for dead on a hundred streets of this city
but oh that captain marvel glance
brushing up against my skull like a steel bar
in passing
and my heart withered sheets in the gutter
passing passing
booted feet and bus drivers
and old yentes in Brighton Beach kitchens
SHIT! said the king and the whole court strained
passing
me out as an ill-tempered wind
lashing around the corner
of 125th Street and Lenox.

Keyfood

In the Keyfood Market on Broadway
a woman waits
by the window
daily and patient
the comings and goings of buyers
neatly labeled old
like yesterday's bread
her restless experienced eyes
weigh fears like grapefruit
testing for ripeness.

Once in the market
she was more
comfortable than wealthy
more black than white
more proper than friendly
more rushed than alone
all her powers defined her
like a carefully kneaded loaf
rising and restrained
working and making loving
behind secret eyes.

Once she was all
the sums of her knowing
counting on her to sustain them
once she was more
somebody else's mother than mine
now she weighs faces
as once she weighed grapefruit.

Waiting
she does not count her change
Her lonely eyes measure
all who enter the market
are they new
are they old
enough
can they buy each other?

A Trip On The Staten Island Ferry

Dear Jonno
there are pigeons who nest
on the Staten Island Ferry
and raise their young
between the moving decks
and never touch
ashore.

Every voyage is a journey.

Cherish this city
left you by default
include it in your daydreams
there are still
secrets
in the streets
even I have not discovered
who knows
if the old men
who shine shoes on the Staten Island Ferry
carry their world
in a box slung across their shoulders
if they share their lunch
with birds
flying back and forth
upon an endless journey
if they ever find their way
back home.

My Fifth Trip To Washington
Ended In Northeast Delaware

for CC—Ring Around Congress June, 1972

Halfway between the rain and Washington
as we stopped stuck in the middle of Delaware and a deluge
At least she said
as the muddy waters rose covering our good intentions
At least she said
as we sat stranded neither dry nor high enough
somewhere over a creek very busy becoming a river
somewhere in northeast Delaware
At least she said
as we waited for the engine
to tug us back to where we had started from
and my son complained he could have had more fun
wrapped up in an envelope
At least she said
as the flooded out tracks receded and the waters rose around
     us
and the children fussed and fretted but were really
very brave about it
and the windows started to leak in on our shoes
and the gum and the games and the New York Times
and the chocolate bars and the toilet paper
all ran out
as the frozen fruit juice melted
and the mayonnaise in the tuna fish went sour
At least she said
as the rain kept falling down
and we couldn't get through to Washington
as we slumped
damp and disappointed in our rumpled up convictions
At least she said
The Indians Aren't Attacking.

Now

Woman power
is
Black power
is
Human power
is
always feeling
my heart beats
as my eyes open
as my hands move
as my mouth speaks

I am
are you

Ready.

To The Girl Who Lives In A Tree

A letter in my mailbox says you've made it
to Honduras and I wonder what is the colour
of the wood you are chopping now.

When you left this city I wept for a year
down 14th Street across the Taconic Parkway
through the shingled birdcotes along Riverside Drive
and I was glad because in your going
you left me a new country
where Riverside Drive became an embattlement
that even dynamite could not blast free
where making both love and war became less inconsistent
and as my tears watered morning I became
my own place to fathom
While part of me follows you still thru the woods of Oregon
splitting dead wood with a rusty axe
acting out the nightmares of your mothers
creamy skin soot-covered from communal fires
where you provide and labour to discipline your dreams
whose symbols are immortalized in lies of history
told like fairy tales called power
behind the throne called noble frontier drudge and
we both know you are not white
with rage or fury but only from bleeding
too much while trudging behind a wagon and confidentially
did you really conquer Donner Pass with only a handcart?

My mothers nightmares are not yours but just as binding.
If in your sleep you tasted a child's blood on your teeth
while your chained black hand could not rise
to wipe away his death upon your lips
perhaps you would consider then
why I choose this brick and shitty stone
over the good earth's challenge of green.

Your mothers nightmares are not mine but just as binding.
We share more than a trap between our legs
where long game howl back and forth across country
finding less than what they bargained for
but more than they ever feared
so dreams or not, I think you will be back soon from Honduras
where the woods are even thicker than in Oregon.
You will see it finally as a choice too
between loving women or loving trees
and if only from the standpoint of free movement
women win
hands down.

Barren

Your lashes leave me naked in the square.
But I have bled on prouder streets than these
so, my executioner, beware!
The song that haunts you through the trees
as you ride home to comfort
will not leave you at your door.
The warm maid brushing back her hair
who greets you with a kiss
knows my tune well,
and hums it under-breath
while your wine sours in your cup.
Smiling, she serves your dinner up
and need not ask what sound your ear
mulls over and over
like witches laughter
nor whom it was
your rope cut in the square.

Her tongue
has tasted your death many nights
while you asleep beside her
dreamed me
your tormentor.

But she and I have come this way
before.

Hard Love Rock #II

Listen brother love you
love you love you love you dig me
a different coloured grave
we are both lying
side by side in the same place
where you put me
down
deeper still
we are
aloneness unresolved by weeping
sacked cities not rebuilt
by slogans
by rhetorical pricks
picking the lock
that has always been
open.

Black is
not beautiful baby
beautiful baby beautiful
lets do it again
It is

not
being screwed twice
at the same time
from on top
as well as
from my side.

Memorial IV

As my heart burned
I discovered memory
turning the sky to dust
your death
into a simple prayer
for rain
and now
remembering you
slowly
becomes a ritual
robbing us both.
New fires move
between me and your sacred face
flashing
on and off in the corners of snapshots
and in tonight's weather report
where I heard
echoes of your name
spelled backward.

I thought I could discover you
in myself
as I wakened
your name still on my tongue
haunting my own life
without regret or sorrow
but nothing
is more cruel
than waiting and hoping
an answer will come.

Love Poem

Speak earth and bless me with what is richest
make sky flow honey out of my hips
rigid as mountains
spread over a valley
carved out by the mouth of rain.

And I knew when I entered her I was
high wind in her forests hollow
fingers whispering sound
honey flowed
from the split cup
impaled on a lance of tongues
on the tips of her breasts on her navel
and my breath
howling into her entrances
through lungs of pain.

Greedy as herring-gulls
or a child
I swing out over the earth
over and over
again.

Mentor

Scaling your words like crags I found
silence
speaking in a mouthful of sun
and I say you are young
for your lips are not stone
to the rain's fall
I say you are lovely to speak
in a mouthful of sun
nor does summer await you.

I see the midnight
heavy as windows sealed against fire
and the tears
coiled like snakes in your eyes
I see your forehead like snow
and the names of the so many winters
your fingers play over
plucking out rays of light
to anoint me home;

Yet I say you are young
and your lips are not stone
to be weathered
rather a song
learned when my aprils were fallow.
I sing this for beacon now
lighting us home
each to our separate house.

The Fallen

M'lord, the stars no longer
concern themselves with you.
                    Druon

Bright uncanny music was beating through the room.
We had come
afraid
to seek some long range
and less threatening death
for us
but the coffee fouled with memory
and I spoke through a mouth
of unshed tears.
Your wild hair curled about your eyes
like commas
in a poem I could not read.
Our words fell
crumpled empty circles
and the beating rain outside
told far more truth.

Separation

The stars dwindle
and will not reward me
even in triumph.

It is possible
to shoot a man
in self defense
and still notice
how his red blood
decorates the snow.

Even

Nothing
is sorry
sameness
a trap called
no dream remembered.

There are no iron creases
in the mind's coat
no past season's shelter
against tonight's rain
every stain
the same
sin of unlonging
lying
pouring
like windless brown rags
of summer falling
away from the trees.

Memorial III
From A Phone Booth On
Broadway

Some time turns inside out
and the whole day collapses into
a desperate search
for a telephone booth that works
for
    quick quick
             I must call you
who has not spoken inside my head
for over a year
but now surely if this phone burrs
long enough
pressed up against my ear
you will blossom back into sound
you will answer
must answer
answer me answer me
answer goddammit
answer
        please
answer
this is the last time
I shall ever call
you.

And Don't Think
I Won't Be Waiting

I am supposed to say
it doesn't matter look me up some
time when you're in my neighborhood
needing
a drink or some books good talk
a quick dip before lunch—
but I never was one
for losing
what I couldn't afford
from the beginning
your richness made my heart
burn like a roman candle.

Now I don't mind
your hand on my face like fire
like a slap
turned inside out
quick as a caress
but I'm warning you
this time
you will not slip away
under a covering cloud
of my tears.

For My Singing Sister

Little sister, not all black
people are all ready
people
are not always black
people
finding them
selves close
to how they see
themselves
being most important.

I see your friends are
young skinny girls sometimes
tall sometimes slight sometimes
beige and neutral or mean or honest or weak
sometimes warm some
times even you
haunted by fat black women who alter
like dreams in a shattered mirror
becoming
sometimes tall sometimes slight sometimes
beige and neutral or mean
honest or weak sometimes warm
sometimes even you
hiding in a bloodbath of color
as you slice up love
on the edge of your little mirrors
making smaller
but not safer
images of your sun.

Cherish your nightmare
sister
or under a cloak of respect
the fat black witch
may be buried
with a silver stake
through your heart.

Monkeyman

There is a strange man attached to my backbone
who thinks he can sap me or break me
if he bleaches out my son my water my fire
if he confuses my tongue by shitting his symbols
into my words.

Every day I walk out of my house
with this curious weight on my back
peering out from between my ear and my shoulder
and each time I move my head
his breath smells like a monkey
he tugs at my short hairs
trying to make me look
into shop windows
trying to make me buy
wigs and girdles and polyutherane pillows
and whenever
I walk through Harlem
he whispers—"be careful—
"our nigger will get us!"

I used to pretend
I did not hear him.

Naturally

Since Naturally Black is Naturally Beautiful
I must be proud
and, naturally,
Black and
Beautiful
who always was a trifle
yellow
and plain
though proud
before.

So I've given up pomades
having spent the summer sunning
and feeling
naturally
free
(and if I die of skin
   cancer
   oh well—one less
   black and beautiful me)
For no agency spends millions
to prevent my summer's tanning
and nobody trembles nightly
with a fear
of lily cities being swallowed
by a summer ocean
of naturally woolly hair.

But I've bought my can of
Natural Hair Spray—
made and marketed in Watts—
still thinking more
Proud Beautiful Black Women
could better make and use
Black bread.

Song For A Thin Sister

Either heard or taught
as girls
we thought
that skinny was funny
or a little bit
silly
and feeling a pull
toward the large and the colorful
I would joke you
when
you grew too thin.

But your new kind of hunger
makes me chilly
like danger
for I see you forever retreating
shrinking
into a stranger
in flight—
and
growing up
black and fat
I was so sure
that skinny was funny
or silly
but always
white.

Release Time

I came to their white
terror first
the nuns with their ghostly motives
hidden in black
motionless
yet always upon us before we sinned
always knowing
and smiling
sadly.

Was it the neat sample loaves
of stale Silvercup bread
and lukewarm milk
doled out in the chalky afternoons
or the threat of public school always
hanging over us
that made me want to believe
the slight face of magic
marooned in an ocean of black
shaping the words by which I learned

to pray to almighty god to
blessed michael the archangel
defend us in battle be our protection
against the wickedness and snares of
the devil who comes
white robed
to our daily crucifixions
restrain him oh lord we beseech and implore
you
who shall not hear us
pray again
to seek in ourselves what is human
to sustain us
and less terror
for our children.

Revolution Is One Form
Of Social Change

When the man is busy
making niggers
it doesn't matter
much
what shade
you are.

If he runs out of one
particular color
he can always switch
to size
and when he's finished
off the big ones
he'll just change
to sex
which is
after all
where it all began.

Oya

God of my father discovered at midnight
my mother asleep on her thunders
my father
returning at midnight
out of tightening circles of anger
out of days' punishment
the inelegant safety of power
Now midnight empties your house of bravado
and passion sleeps like a mist
outside desire
your strength splits like a melon
dropped on our prisoners floor
midnight glows
like a jeweled love
at the core of the broken fruit.

My mother is sleeping.
Hymns of dream lie like bullets
in her nights weapons
the sacred steeples
of nightmare are secret and hidden
in the disguise of fallen altars
I too shall learn how to conquer yes.
Yes yes god
damned
I love you
now free me
quickly
before I destroy us.

All Hallows Eve

My mother taught each one of us
to pray
as soon as we could talk
and every Halloween
to comfort us
before she went to work
my mother cooked fresh pumpkin with brown sugar
and placing penny candles in our windows
she said her yearly prayers
for all our dead.

As soon as mother left us
we feasted on warm pumpkin
until the empty pot sang out its earthy smell
and then, our mouths free,
we told each other stories of other Halloweens
making our wishes true
while from our windows
we watched the streets grow dark
and the witches slowly gathering below.

In each window
a penny candle in its own dish of water
flickered around our tales
throughout the evening.
Most of them burnt down
before our stories ended
and we went to bed
without replacing them.

Ballad From Childhood

Mommy mommy come and see
what the strawmen left for me
in our land of ice and house of snow
I have found a seed to grow
Mommy may I plant a tree?

What the eyes don't see the heart don't hurt.

But mommy look the seed has wings
my tree might call a bird that sings . . .
true, the strawmen left no spade no earth
and ice will not bring my seed to birth—
but what if I dig beneath these things?

Watch the birds forget but the trap doesn't.

Please mommy do not beat me so!
yes I will learn to love the snow!
yes I want neither seed nor tree!
yes ice is quite enough for me!
who knows what trouble-leaves might grow!

I don't fatten frogs to feed snakes.

Times Change And We
Change With Them Or
We Seem To Have Lost Touch
With Each Other

There are so many girls now in the street
who look like Noelle
who lived behind a green door and a garden
in the heart of the West Village
with waterbugs in her half-kitchen
and a persistent sense of death.

But now they all seem much younger.
They have more and less time to play, to dye
their hair blonde or try yoga
and winnow the chaff from their bodies—
spare in the fashion of today—
which was not quite so in the days of Noelle
and perhaps with luck
that was never Noelle's
these girls may learn to distinguish
their growing grain from a cancer.

Noelle was skinny and strong
and prone to a host of ailments.
After her tenth accident
she began
to develop an ulcer
saw an analyst
who died, and then went into advertising.
Noelle moved out of her green house
into midtown, and had gained weight
the last time I saw her.

Perhaps now she is also dead.

All the young girls who wear her faces
are much cooler now
one can tell right away
they are impregnable.
Most of them know that
a sense of death
is often the sign
of internal bleeding.

To Marie, in Flight

For women
perspective is more easily maintained.

But something in my body
teaches patience
is no virtue
every month
renews its own destruction
while my blood rages
for proof
or continuity.

Peering out of this
pressured metal cabin
I see my body patterns
repeated on the earth
I hear my blood breath beating
through the dark green places
between the mountain's thrust
without judgement or decision
a valley rhythm captures all.

The Bees

In the street outside a school
what the children learn
possesses them.
Little boys yell as they stone a flock of bees
trying to swarm
between the lunchroom window and an iron grate.
The boys sling furious rocks
smashing the windows.
The bees, buzzing their anger,
are slow to attack.
Then one boy is stung
into quicker destruction
and the school guards come
long wooden sticks held out before them
they advance upon the hive
beating the almost finished rooms of wax apart
mashing the new tunnels in
while fresh honey drips
down their broomsticks
and the little boy feet becoming expert
in destruction
trample the remaining and bewildered bees
into the earth.

Curious and apart
four little girls look on in fascination
learning a secret lesson
trying to understand their own destruction.
One girl cries out
"Hey, the bees weren't making any trouble!"
and she steps across the feebly buzzing ruins
to peer up at the empty, grated nook
"We could have studied honey-making!"

Viet-Nam Addenda

for / Clifford

Genocide doesn't only mean bombs
at high noon and the cameras
panning in on the ruptured stomach
of somebody else's pubescent daughter.
A small difference in time and space
names that war
while we live
117th street at high noon
powerlessly familiar.
We are raped of our children
in silence
giving birth to spots quickly
rubbed out at dawn
on the streets of Jamaica
or left
all the time in the world
for the nightmare of idleness
to turn their hands
against us.

Visit To A City
Out Of Time

If St. Louis
took its rhythms
from the river
that cuts through it
the pulse of the Mississippi
has torn this city
apart.

St. Louis is
somebody's home
and not answering
was
nobody
shoveling snow
because spring would come
one day.

In time
people who live
by rivers
dream
they are immortal.

The Brown Menace
Or
Poem To The Survival
of Roaches

Call me
your deepest urge
toward survival
call me
and my brothers and sisters
in the sharp smell of your refusal
call me
roach and presumptious
nightmare on your white pillow
your itch to destroy
the indestructible
part of yourself.

Call me
your own determination
in the most detestable shape
you can become
friend of your image
within me
I am you
in your most deeply cherished nightmare
scuttling through the painted cracks
you create to admit me
into your kitchens
into your fearful midnights
into your values at noon
in your most secret places
with hate
you learn to honor me
by imitation
as I alter—
through your greedy preoccupations

through your kitchen wars
and your poisonous refusal—
to survive.

To survive.
Survive.

Sacrifice

The only hungers left
are the hungers allowed us.

By the light of our sacred street lamps
by whatever maps we are sworn to follow
pleasure will betray us
unless we do what we must do
without
wanting to do it
feel the enemy stone give way in retreat
without pleasure or satisfaction
we look the other way
as our dreams come true
as our bloody hands move over history
writing
we have come
we have done
what we came to do.

Pulling down statues of rock from their high places
we must level the expectation
upon which they stand
waiting for us
to fulfill their image
waiting
for our feet to replace them.

Unless we refuse to sleep
even one night in houses of marble
the sight of our children's false pleasure
will undo us
for our children have grown
in the shadow of what was
the shape of marble
between their eyes and the sun
but we do not wish to stand

like great marble statues
between our children's eyes
and their sun.

Learning all
we can use
only what is vital
The only sacrifice of worth
is the sacrifice of desire.

Blackstudies

I
A chill wind sweeps the high places.
On the ground I watch bearers of wood
carved in the image of old and mistaken gods
labour in search of weapons against the blind dancers
who balance great dolls on their shoulders
as they scramble over the same earth
searching for food.

In a room on the 17th floor my spirit is choosing
I am afraid of speaking
the truth
in a room on the 17th floor
my body is dreaming
it sits
bottom pinned to a table
eating perpetual watermelon inside my own head
while young girls assault my door
with curse rags
stiff with their mothers old secrets
covering up their new promise
with old desires no longer their need
with old satisfactions they never enjoyed
outside my door they are waiting
with questions that feel like judgements
when they are unanswered.

The palms of my hands have black marks running across them.
So are signed makers of myth
who are sworn through our blood to give
legend
children will come to understand
to speak out living words like this poem
that knits truth into fable
to leave my story behind
though I fall through cold wind condemned
to nursing old gods for a new heart

debtless and without colour
while my flesh is covered by mouths
whose noise keeps my real wants secret.

I do not want to lie. I have loved other
tall young women deep into their colour
who now crawl over a bleached earth
bent into questionmarks
ending a sentence of men
who pretended to be brave.
Even this
can be an idle defense
protecting the lies I am trying to reject.

I am afraid
that the mouths I feed will turn against me
will refuse to swallow in the silence
I am warning them to avoid
I am afraid
they will kernel me out like a walnut
extracting the nourishing seed
as my husk stains their lips
with the mixed colours of my pain.

While I sit choosing the voice
in which my children hear my prayers
above the wind
they will follow the black roads out of my hands
unencumbered by the weight of my remembered sorrows
by the weight of my remembered sorrows
they will use my legends to shape their own language
and make it ruler
measuring the distance between my hungers
and their own purpose.
I am afraid
They will discard my most ancient nightmares
where the fallen gods became demon
instead of dust.

II

Just before light devils woke me
trampling my flesh into fruit
that would burst in the sun
until I came to despise every evening
fearing a strange god at the fall of each night
and when my mother punished me
by sending me to bed without my prayers
I had no names for darkness.

I do not know whose words protected me
whose tales or tears prepared me
for this trial on the 17th floor
I do not know whose legends blew
through my mothers furies
but somehow they fell through my sleeping lips
like the juice of forbidden melons
and the little black seeds were sown
throughout my heart
like closed and waiting eyes
and although demons rode me
until I rose up a child of morning
deep roads sprouted over the palms
of my hidden fists
dark and growing.

III

Chill winds swirl around these high blank places.
It is the time when the bearer of hard news
is destroyed for the message
when it is heard.
A. B. is a poet who says our people
fear our own beauty
has not made us hard enough
to survive victory
but he too has written his children upon women
I hope with love.
I bear mine alone in the mouth of the enemy

upon a desk on the 17th floor
swept bare by cold winds
bright as neon.

IV

Their demon father rode me just before daylight
I learned his tongue as he reached
for my hands at dawn
before he could touch the palms of my hands
to devour my children
I learned his language
I ate him
and left his bones mute in the noon sun.

Now all the words in my legend come garbled
except anguish.
Visions of chitterlings I never ate
strangle me in a nightmare of leaders
at crowded meetings to study our problems
I move awkward and ladylike
through four centuries of unused bathtubs
that never smile
not even an apologetic grin
I worry on nationalist holidays
make a fetish of lateness
with limp unbelieved excuses
shunning the use of pronouns
as an indirect assult
what skin I have left
unbetrayed by scouring
uncovered by mouths that shriek
but do not speak my real wants
glistens and twinkles blinding all beholders
"But I just washed them, Mommy!"

Only the black marks on my hands itch and flutter
shredding my words and wherever they fall
the earth springs up denials
that I pay for

only the dark roads over my palms
wait for my voice
to follow.

V

The chill wind is beating down from the high places.
My students wait outside my door
searching condemning listening
for what I am sworn to tell them
for what they least want to hear
clogging the only exit from the 17th floor
begging in their garbled language
beyond judgement or understanding
"oh speak to us now mother for soon
we will not need you
only your memory
teaching us questions."

Stepping into my self
I open the door
and leap groundward
wondering
what shall they carve for weapons
what shall they grow for food.

COAL

(1976)

To the People of Sun,
That We May All
Better Understand

If we run fast enough
the winds will not catch us.
—Beth Rollins

Rites of Passage

Now rock the boat to a fare-thee-well.
Once we suffered dreaming
into the place where the children are playing
their child's games
where the children are hoping
knowledge survives if
unknowing
they follow the game
without winning.

Their fathers are dying
back to the freedom of wise children
playing at knowing
their fathers are dying
whose deaths will not free them
of growing from knowledge
of knowing
when the game becomes foolish
a dangerous pleading
for time out of power.

Quick
children kiss us
we are growing
through dream.

Father Son and Holy Ghost

I have not ever seen my father's grave.

Not that his judgement eyes have been
forgotten
nor his great hands' print
on our evening doorknobs
    one half turn each night
    and he would come
    drabbled with the world's business
    massive and silent as the whole day's wish
    ready to redefine each of our shapes—
but that now the evening doorknobs wait
and do not recognize us as we pass.

Each week a different woman—
regular as his one quick glass each evening—
pulls up the grass his stillness grows
calling it weed. Each week
A different woman has my mother's face
and he, who time has,
changeless,
must be amazed
who knew and loved but one.

My father died in silence, loving creation
and well-defined response.
He lived
still judgements on familiar things
and died
knowing a January 15th that year me.

Lest I go into dust
I have not ever seen my father's grave.

Coal

I
is the total black, being spoken
from the earth's inside.
There are many kinds of open
how a diamond comes into a knot of flame
how sound comes into a word, coloured
by who pays what for speaking.

Some words are open like a diamond
on glass windows
singing out within the passing crash of sun
Then there are words like stapled wagers
in a perforated book,—buy and sign and tear apart—
and come whatever wills all chances
the stub remains
an ill-pulled tooth with a ragged edge.
Some words live in my throat
breeding like adders. Others know sun
seeking like gypsies over my tongue
to explode through my lips
like young sparrows bursting from shell.
Some words
bedevil me.

Love is a word, another kind of open.
As the diamond comes into a knot of flame
I am Black because I come from the earth's inside
now take my word for jewel in the open light.

Rooming Houses Are Old Women

Rooming houses are old women
rocking dark windows into their whens
waiting incomplete circles
rocking
rent office to stoop to
community bathrooms to gas rings and
under-bed boxes of once useful garbage
city issued with a twice monthly check
and the young men next door
with their loud midnight parties
and fishy rings left in the bathtub
no longer arouse them
from midnight to mealtime no stops inbetween
light breaking to pass through jumbled up windows
and who was it who married the widow that Buzzie's son
    messed with?

To Welfare and insult from the slow shuffle
from dayswork to shopping bags
heavy with leftovers

Rooming houses
are old women waiting
searching
through darkening windows
the end or beginning of agony
old women seen through half-ajar doors
hoping
they are not waiting
but being
the entrance to somewhere
unknown and desired
but not new.

The Woman Thing

The hunters are back from beating the winter's face
in search of a challenge or task
in search of food
making fresh tracks for their children's hunger
they do not watch the sun
they cannot wear its heat for a sign
of triumph or freedom;
The hunters are treading heavily homeward
through snow that is marked
with their own bloody footprints.
emptyhanded, the hunters return
snow-maddened, sustained by their rages.

In the night after food they may seek
young girls for their amusement. But now
the hunters are coming
and the unbaked girls flee from their angers.
All this day I have craved
food for my child's hunger
Emptyhanded the hunters come shouting
injustices drip from their mouths
like stale snow melted in sunlight.

Meanwhile
the woman thing my mother taught me
bakes off its covering of snow
like a rising blackening sun.

Oaxaca

Beneath the carving drag of wood
the land moves slowly.
But lightning comes.

Growing their secret in brown earth
spread like a woman
daring
is weary work for still-eyed men
who break the earth
nursing their seed
and a hard watch through the dry season.
Yet at the edge of bright thin day
past the split plow—they look
to the hills—to the brewing thunder
for the storm is known.

The land moves slowly.
Though the thunder's eve
can crack with a flash
the glass-brittle crust of a mountains face
the land moves slowly.
All a man's strength in his son's arms
to carve one sleeve
into rock defiant earth
and the spread land waits.

Slow long the plowing
through dry-season brown
and the land moves slowly.

But lightning comes.

Summer Oracle

Without expectation
there is no end
to the shocks of morning
or even a small summer.

Now the image is fire
blackening the vague lines
into defiance across the city.
the image is fire
sun warming us in a cold country
barren of symbols for love.

But I have forsaken order
and imagine you into fire
untouchable in a magician's cloak
covered with signs of destruction and birth
sewn with griffins and arrows and hammers
and gold sixes stitched into your hem.
your fingers draw fire
but still the old warlocks shun you
for no gourds ring in your sack
no spells bring forth peace
and I am still fruitless and hungry
this summer
the peaches are flinty and juiceless
and cry sour worms.

The image is fire
flaming over you burning off excess
like the blaze planters start
to burn off bagasse from the canefields
after a harvest.

The image is fire
the high sign that rules our summer
I smell it in the charred breezes blowing over

your body
close
hard
essential
under its cloak of lies.

Generation

How the young attempt and are broken
differs from age to age
We were brown free girls
love singing beneath our skin
sun in our hair in our eyes
sun our fortune
and the wind had made us golden
made us gay.

In a season of limited power
we wept out our promises
And these are the children we try now
for temptations that wear our face.
But who comes back from our latched cities of falsehood
to warn them that the road to nowhere
is slippery with our blood
to warn them
they need not drink the river to get home
since we have purchased bridges
with our mothers' bloody gold;—
for now we are more than kin
who come to share
not only blood
but the bloodiness of our failures.

How the young are tempted and betrayed
into slaughter or conformity
is a turn of the mirror
time's question only.

A Family Resemblance

My sister has my hair my mouth my eyes
and I presume her trustless.
When she was young and open to any fever
wearing gold like a veil of fortune on her face
she waited through each rain a dream of light.
But the sun came up
burning our eyes like crystal
bleaching the sky of promise and
my sister stood
Black, unblessed and unbelieving
shivering in the first cold show of love.

I saw her gold become an arch
where nightmare hunted
down the porches of restless night.
Now through echoes of denial
she walks a bleached side of reason.
Secret now
my sister never waits
nor mourns the gold that wandered from her bed.

My sister has my tongue
and all my flesh
unanswered
and I presume her trustless
as a stone.

Song

The wild trees have bought me
and will sell you a wind
in the forest of falsehoods
where your search must not end

for their roots are not wise.
Strip our loving of dream
pay its secrets to thunder
and ransom me home.

Beware oaks in laughter
know hemlock is lying
when she sings of defiance.
The sand words she is saying

will sift over and bury
while the pale moons I hate
seduce you in phases
through oceans of light.

And the wild trees shall sell me
for their safety from lightning
to sand that will flay me
for the next evening's planting.

They will fill my limp skin
with wild dreams from their root
and grow from my flesh
new handfuls of hate

till our ransom is wasted
and the morning speaks out
in a thin voice of wisdom
that loves me too late.

On a Night of the Full Moon

I

Out of my flesh that hungers
and my mouth that knows
comes the shape I am seeking
for reason.
The curve of your waiting body
fits my waiting hand
your breasts warm as sunlight
your lips quick as young birds
between your thighs the sweet
sharp taste of limes.

Thus I hold you
frank in my heart's eye
in my skin's knowing
as my fingers conceive your flesh
I feel your stomach
moving against me.

Before the moon wanes again
we shall come together.

II

And I would be the moon
spoken over your beckoning flesh
breaking against reservations
beaching thought
my hands at your high tide
over and under inside you
and the passing of hungers
attended, forgotten.

Darkly risen
the moon speaks
my eyes
judging your roundness
delightful.

Now That I Am Forever with Child

How the days went
while you were blooming within me
I remember each upon each—
the swelling changed planes of my body
and how you first fluttered, then jumped
and I thought it was my heart.

How the days wound down
and the turning of winter
I recall, with you growing heavy
against the wind. I thought
now her hands
are formed, and her hair
has started to curl
now her teeth are done
now she sneezes.
Then the seed opened
I bore you one morning just before spring
My head rang like a fiery piston
my legs were towers between which
A new world was passing.

Since then
I can only distinguish
one thread within running hours
You, flowing through selves
toward You.

What My Child Learns of the Sea

What my child learns of the sea
of the summer thunders
of the riddles that hide in the curve of spring
she will learn in my twilights
and childlike
revise every autumn.

What my child learns
as her winters grow into time
has ripened in my own body
to enter her eyes with first light.

This is why
more than blood
or the milk I have given
one day a strange girl will step
to the back of a mirror
cutting my ropes
of sea and thunder and spring.
Of the way she will taste her autumns—
toast-brittle or warmer than sleep—
and the words she will use for winter
I stand already condemned.

Spring People

for Jonno

What anger in my hard-won bones
or heritage of water
makes me reject the april
and fear to walk upon the earth
in spring?

At springtime and evening
I recall how we came
like new thunder
beating the earth
leaving the taste of rain and sunset
all our hungers before us.
Away from the peace of half truths
and springtime passing unsaid
we came in the touch of fire
came to the sun
lay with a wild earth
until spent and knowing
we brought forth our young.

Now insolent aprils bedevil us—
earthy conceits—
to remind us that all else is forfeit
only our blood-hungry children
remember
what face we had
what startling eyes.

Poem for a Poet

I think of a coffin's quiet
when I sit in the world of my car
separate and observing
with the windows closed and washed clean
by the rain. I like to sit there
watching the other worlds pass. Yesterday evening
I sat in my car on Sheridan Square
flat and broke and a little bit damp
thinking about money and rain and how
the Village broads with their narrow hips
rolled like drunken shovels
down Christopher Street.

Then I saw you unmistakeably
darting out from between a police car and
what used to be Atkin's all-night diner—
where we sat making bets the last time I saw you
on how many busts we could count through the plateglass window
in those last skinny hours before dawn
with our light worded-out but still burning
and the earlier evening's promise dregs in our coffee cups—
and I saw you dash out and turn left at the corner
your beard spiky with rain and refusing
shelter under your chin.

But I had thought you were dead Jarrell
struck down by a car at sunset on a North Carolina road
or were you the driver
tricked into a fatal swerve by some twilit shadow
or was that Frank O'Hara
or Conrad Kent Rivers
and you
the lonely spook in a Windy City motel
draped in the secrets of your convulsive death
all alone

all poets all loved and dying alone
that final death
less real than those deaths you lived
and for which I forgave you?

I watched you hurry down Fourth Street Jarrell
from the world of my car in the rain
remembering that Spring Festival Night
at Womens College in North Carolina
and wasn't that world a coffin's retreat
of spring whispers romance and rhetoric
Untouched
by the wind buffeting up the road from Greensboro
and nobody mentioned the Black Revolution
or Sit-Ins or Freedom Rides or SNCC
or cattle-prods in Jackson Mississippi—
where I was to find myself how many years later:

You were mistaken that night and I told you
later in a letter beginning—Dear Jarrell
if you sit in one place long enough
the whole world will pass you by . . .
you were wrong when you said I took
living too seriously
meaning you were afraid I might take you
too seriously
you shouldn't have worried because
although I dug you too much
to put you down
I never took you at all
except as a good piece of my first journey south
except as I take you now
gladly and separate at a distance
and wondering
as I have so often
how come being so cool
you weren't also a little bit
black.

And also why you have returned
to this dying city
and what piece of me is it then
buried down there in North Carolina.

Story Books on a Kitchen Table

Out of her womb of pain my mother spat me
into her ill-fitting harness of despair
into her deceits
where anger re-conceived me
piercing my eyes like arrows
pointed by her nightmare
of who I was not
becoming.

Going away
she left in her place
iron maidens to protect me
and for my food
the wrinkled milk of legend
where I wandered through the lonely rooms of afternoon
wrapped in nightmares
from the Orange and Red and Yellow
Purple and Blue and Green
Fairy Books
where White witches ruled
over the empty kitchen table
and never wept
or offered gold
nor any kind enchantment
for the vanished mother
of a black girl.

Pirouette

I saw
your hands on my lips like blind needles
blunted
from sewing up stone
and
    where are you from
                you said
your hands reading over my lips for
some road through uncertain night
for your feet to examine home
where are you from
                you said
your hands
on my lips like thunder
promising rain

a land where all lovers are mute.

And
    why are you weeping
                you said
your hands in my doorway like rainbows
following rain
why are you weeping?

I am come home.

Hard Love Rock

Today I heard my heart screeching like a subway train
loudly enough to remind me it was still human
loudly enough to hurt
but telling me still
you were a ghost I had
better left in the cradle,
telling me still
that our tracks ran around
instead of straight out past the sewers
that I would have nothing for barter left
not even the print of love's grain
pressed into my flesh from our wooden cross
left splintered and shapeless
after the slaughter.

And when it was over
only pain.

Father the Year Has Fallen

Father the year has fallen.
Leaves bedeck my careful flesh like stone.
One shard of brilliant summer pierced me
and remains.
By this only
unregenerate bone
I am not dead, but waiting.
When the last warmth is gone
I shall bear in the snow.

Gemini

Moon minded the sun goes farther from us
split into swirled days, smoked,
unhungered, and unkempt
no longer young.

All the earth falls down
like lost light frightened out between my fingers.
Here at the end of night
our love is a burnt out ocean
a dry worded, brittle bed.
Our roots, once nourished by the cool lost water
cry out—"Remind us!"—and the oyster world
cries out its pearls like tears.

And was this the wild calling I heard in the long night past
wrapped in a stone closed house?
I wakened to moon and the sound breached dark
and thinking a new word spoken—
some promise made—
broke through the screaming night
seeking a gateway out

But the night was dark
and love was a burning fence about my house.

Bridge through My Window

In curve scooped out and necklaced with light
burst pearls stream down my out-stretched arms to earth.
Oh bridge my sister bless me before I sleep
the wild air is lengthening
and I am tried beyond strength or bearing
over water.

Love, we are both shorelines
a left country
where time suffices
and the right land
where pearls roll into earth and spring up day.
joined, our bodies have passage into one
without merging
as this slim necklace is anchored into night.

And while the we conspires
to make secret its two eyes
we search the other shore
for some crossing home.

Conversations in Crisis

I speak to you as a friend speaks
or a true lover
not out of friendship nor love
but for a clear meeting
of self upon self
in sight of our hearth
but without fire.

I cherish your words that ring
like late summer thunders
to sing without octave
and fade, having spoken the season.
But I hear the false heat of this voice
as it dries up the sides of your words
coaxing melodies from your tongue
and this curled music is treason.

Must I die in your fever—
or, as the flames wax, take cover
in your heart's culverts
crouched like a stranger
under the scorched leaves of your other burnt loves
until the storm passes over?

The Maiden

Once I was immortal beside an ocean
having the names of night
and the first men came
with sledges of fire
driving the sun.

I was brought forth in the moonpit of a virgin
condemned to light
to a dry world's endless mornings
sweeping the moon away
and wherever I fled
seeking a new road home
morning had harrowed the endless rivers
to nest in the dried out bed
of my mother sea.

Time drove the moon down to crescent
and they found me
mortal
beside a moon's crater
mouthing the ocean names of night.

When the Saints
Come Marching in

Plentiful sacrifice and believers in redemption
are all that is needed
so any day now
I expect some new religion
to rise up like tear gas
from the streets of New York
erupting like the rank pavement smell
released by the garbage-trucks'
baptismal drizzle.

The high priests have been ready and waiting
with their incense pans full of fire.
I do not know the rituals
the exhaltations
nor what name of the god
the survivors will worship
I only know she will be terrible
and very busy
and very old.

On Midsummer's Eve

Ride the swing season
hawk gander or stallion
evading the light
you survive
lost
among the stiff trees
laying rebellious eggs
that roll and splatter
in your enemy sun.

your arrows rot
in a muddy quiver
while the quick vowels
flutter and plummet
through stiff trees without echo
you do not fly.
you do not fly.

Your words explode
under silence
returning
to rot
in the changing season
I ride with the sun
passing
returning again
and again
you do not learn
you do not learn.

Dreams Bite

I

Dreams bite.
The dreamer and his legends
arm at the edge of purpose.

Waking
I see the people of winter
put off their masks
to stain the earth red with blood
while
on the outer edges of sleep
the people of sun
are carving
their own children
into monuments
of war.

II

When I am absolute
at once
with the black earth
fire
I make
my nows
and power is spoken
peace
at rest and
hungry means never
or alone
I shall love
again

When I am obsolete.

Suspension

We entered silence
before the clock struck.

Red wine into crystal
is not quite
fallen
air solidifies around your mouth
once-wind has sucked the curtains in
like fright against the evening wall
prepared for storm   before the room
exhales   your lips
unfold.
Within their sudden opening
I hear
the clock begin
to speak again.

I remember now with the filled crystal
shattered, the wind-whipped curtains
bound and the cold storm
finally broken
how the room felt
when
your word was spoken—

Warm
as the center of your palm
and as unfree.

A Child
Shall Lead

I have a child
whose feet are blind
on every road
but silence.

My boy has
lovely foolish lips
but cannot find
his way to sun

And I am grown
past knowledge.

Afterlove

In what had been a pathway
inbetween
our bed and a shared bathroom
broken hours lap at my heels
reaching my toothbrush
finally
I see
wide valleys filled with water
folding into myself
alone
I cross them into the shower
the tiles right themselves
in retreat
my skin thrills
bruised and battered
as thunderspray splatters
plasma on my horizons
when no more rain comes
I cast me out lightly
returning
on tiptoe
shifting and lurching
against my eyes
plastic curtains
I hung
last December
watching the sun flee
through patterns
spinning
always and never
returning
I spiced my armpits
courting the solstice
and never once did I abandon
believing
I would contrive
to make my world
whole again.

The Dozens

Nothing says that you must see me in the street
with us so close together at that red light
that a blind man could have smelled his grocer—
and nothing says that you must
say hello
as we pass in the street,
but we have known each other too well
in the dark
for this,
and it hurts me when you do not speak.

And no one you were with was quite so fine
that I won't remember this and
suffer you in turn and
in my own fashion which is certainly
not in the street.
For I can count on my telephone
ringing some evening and you
exploding into my room through the receiver
kissing and licking my ear. . . .

I hope you will learn your thing
at least
from some of those spiteful noseless
people who surround you
before the centipede in you
runs out of worlds
one for each foot.

And What About
the Children

Now we've made a child.
and the dire predictions
have changed into wild
grim
speculations;
still the negatives
are waiting
watching
and the relatives
keep right on
Touching . . .
    and how much curl
    is right for a girl?
But if it is said
at some future date
that my son's head
is on straight
he won't care
about his
hair
nor give a damn
whose wife
I am.

For the King and
Queen of Summer

The land of flowers is dusty
and covered with jewels.
Alan writes that Ceylon
is heavy with topaz and rubies
and the stink of rotting lotus.

He will return
with opals and moonstones
around his neck
and a crippled monkey named Buddha
in his back pocket.

When he comes home
the Red Queen
will cook rice-cream and pray
for a second coming
as she fiercely shields the children
until their bones grow stronger.

She teaches them royal forebearance
while the crippled monkey
quite at home
picks his nose
as he makes a shithouse
under their throne.

Fantasy and Conversation

Speckled frogs leap from my mouth
to drown in the coffee
between our wisdoms
and decision.

I could smile
and turn these frogs to pearls
speak of love, our making
our giving.
And if the spell works
shall I break down
or build what is broken
into a new house
shook with confusion

Shall I strike
before our magic
turns colour?

Paperweight

Paper is neither kind nor cruel
merely white in its neutrality
I have for reality now
the brown bar of my arm
moving in broken rhythm
across this dead place.

All the poems I have ever written
are historical reviews of some now-absorbed country
a small judgement
hawking and coughing them up
I have ejected them not unlike children.
Now my throat is clear
and perhaps I shall speak again.

All the poems I have ever written
make a small book shaped like another me
called by yesterday's names
the shedding of a past in patched conceits
moulted like snake skin—
a book of leavings.
I can do anything with them I wish
I can love them or hate them
use them for comfort or warmth
tissues or decoration
dolls or japanese baskets
blankets or spells.
I can use them for magic
lanterns or music
advice or small council
for napkins or past-times or
disposable diapers
I can make fire from them
or kindling
songs or paper chains

Or fold them all into a paper fan
with which to cool my husband's dinner.

Martha

I

Martha this is a catalog of days
passing before you looked again.
Someday you will browse and order them
at will, or in your necessities.

I have taken a house at the Jersey shore
this summer. It is not my house.
Today the lightning bugs came.

On the first day you were dead.
With each breath the skin of your face moved
falling in like crumpled muslin.
We scraped together the smashed image of flesh
preparing a memory. No words.
No words.

On the eighth day
you startled the doctors
speaking from your deathplace
to reassure us that you were trying.

Martha these are replacement days
should you ever need them
given for those you once demanded and never found.
May this trip be rewarding;
no one can fault you again Martha
for answering necessity too well
and the gods who honor hard work
will keep this second coming
free from that lack of choice
which hindered your first journey
to this Tarot house.

They said
no hope no dreaming
accept this case of flesh as evidence
of life without fire

and wrapped you in an electric blanket
kept ten degrees below life.
Fetal hands curled inward on the icy sheets
your bed was so cold
the bruises could not appear.

On the second day I knew you were alive
because the grey flesh of your face
suffered.

I love you and cannot feel you less than Martha
I love you and cannot split this shaved head
from Martha's pushy straightness
asking
in a smash of mixed symbols
How long must I wander here
in this final house of my father?

On the Solstice I was in Providence.
You know this town because you visited friends here.
It trained in Providence on the Solstice—
I remember we passed through here twice
on route Six through Providence to the Cape
where we spent our second summer
trying for peace or equity, even.
It always seemed to be raining
by the time we got to Providence.
The Kirschenbaums live in Providence
and Blossom and Barry
and Frances. And Frances.
Martha I am in love again.
Listen, Frances, I said on the Solstice
our summer has started.
Today we are witches and with enough energy
to move mountains back.
Think of Martha.

Back in my hideous city
I saw you today. Your hair has grown
and your armpits are scented

by some careful attendant.
Your *Testing testing testing*
explosive syllables warning me
Of *The mountain has fallen into dung*—
no Martha remember remember Martha—
Warning
Dead flowers will not come to your bed again.
The sun has started south
our season is over.

Today you opened your eyes, giving
a blue-filmed history to your mangled words.
They help me understand
how you are teaching yourself to learn
again.

I need you need me
Je suis Martha I do not speak french kissing
Oh Wow. Black and . . . Black and . . . beautiful?
Black and becoming
somebody else maybe Erica maybe who sat
in the fourth row behind us in high school
but I never took French with you Martha
and who is this *Madame Erudite*
who is not me?

I find you today in a womb full of patients
blue-robed in various convalescences.
Your eyes are closed you are propped
into a wheelchair, cornered,
in a parody of resting.
The bright glue of tragedy plasters all eyes
to a television set in the opposite corner
where a man is dying
step by step
in the american ritual going.
Someone has covered you
for this first public appearance
in a hospital gown, a badge of your next step.
Evocative voices flow from the set

and the horror is thick
in this room full of broken and mending receptions.

But no one has told you what it's all about Martha
someone has shot another Kennedy
we are drifting closer to what you predicted
and your darkness is indeed speaking
Robert Kennedy is dying Martha
but not you not you not you
he has a bullet in his brain Martha
surgery was never considered for you
since there was no place to start
and no one intended to run you down on a highway
being driven home at 7:30 on a low summer evening
I gave a reading in Harlem that night
and who shall we try for this shaven head now
in the courts of heart Martha
where his murder is televised over and over
with residuals
they have caught the man who shot Robert Kennedy
who was another one of difficult journeys—
he has a bullet in his brain Martha
and much less of a chance than you.

On the first day of July you warned me again
the threads are broken
you darkened into explosive angers and
refused to open your eyes, humming interference
your thoughts are not over Martha
they are you and their task is
to remember Martha
we can help with the other
the mechanics of blood and bone
and you cut through the pain of my words
to warn me again
testing testing whoever passes
must tear out their hearing aids
for the duration.
I hear you explaining Neal
my husband whoever must give me a present

he has to give me
himself where I can find him for
where can be look at himself
in the mirror I am making
or over my bed where the window
is locked into battle with a wall?

Now I sit in New Jersey with lightning bugs and mosquitoes
typing and thinking of you.
Tonight you started seizures
which they say is a temporary relapse
but this lake is far away Martha
and I sit unquiet in New Jersey
thinking of you
I Ching the Book of Changes
says I am impertinent to ask of you obliquely
but I have no direct question
only need.
When I cast an oracle today
it spoke of the Abyssmal again
which of all the Hexagrams
is very difficult but very promising
in it water finds its own level, flowing
out from the lowest point.
And I cast another also that cautioned
the superior man to seek his strength
only in its own season.
Martha what did we learn from our brief season
when the summer grackles rang in my walls?
one and one is too late now
you journey through darkness alone
leafless I sit far from my present house
and the grackles' voices are dying
we shall love each other here if ever at all.

II
Yes foolish prejudice lies
I hear you Martha
that you would never harm my children
but you have forgotten their names

and that you are Elizabeth's godmother.
And you offer me coral rings, watches
even your body
if I will help you sneak home.

No Martha my blood is not muddy my hands
are not dirty to touch
Martha I do not know your night nurse's name
even though she is black
yes I did live in Brighton Beach once
which is almost Rockaway
one bitter winter
but not with your night nurse Martha
and yes I agree this is one hell
of a summer.

No you cannot walk yet Martha
and no the medicines you are given
to quiet your horrors
have not affected your brain
yes it is very hard to think but
it is getting easier and yes Martha
we have loved each other and yes I hope
we still can
no Martha I do not know if we shall ever
sleep in each other's arms again.

III
It is the middle of August and you are alive
to discomfort. You have been moved
into a utility room across the hall
from the critical ward because your screaming
disturbs the other patients
your bedside table has been moved also
which means you will be there for a while
a favorite now with the floor nurses
who put up a sign on the utility room door
I'M MARTHA HERE DO NOT FORGET ME
PLEASE KNOCK.

A golden attendant named Sukie
bathes you as you proposition her
she is very pretty and very gentle.
The frontal lobe of the brain governs inhibitions
the damage is after all slight
and they say the screaming will pass.

Your daughter Dorrie promises you
will be as good as new, Mama
who only wants to be *Bad as the old.*

I want some truth good hard truth
a sign of youth
we were all young once we had
a good thing going
now I'm making a plan
for a dead rabbit a rare rabbit.
I am dying goddammit dying am I
Dying?
Death is a word you can say now
pain is mortal
I am dying for god's sake won't someone please
get me a doctor PLEASE
your screams beat against our faces as you yell
begging relief from the blank cruelty
of a thousand nurses.
A moment of silence breaks
as you accumulate fresh sorrows
then through your pain-fired face
you slip me a wink

Martha Winked.

    IV
Your face straightens into impatience
with the loads of shit you are handed
'You're doing just fine Martha what time is it Martha'
'What did you have for supper tonight Martha'
testing testing whoever passes for Martha
you weary of it.

All the people you must straighten out
pass your bedside in the utility room
bringing you cookies
and hoping
you will be kinder than they were.

Go away Mama and Bubie
for 30 years you made me believe
I was shit you shot out for the asking
but I'm not and you'd better believe it
right now would you kindly
stop rubbing my legs
and GET THE HELL OUT OF HERE.
Next week Bubie bring Teglach
your old favorite
and will you be kinder Martha
then we were to the shell the cocoon
out of which the you is emerging?

V
No one you were can come so close
to death without dying
into another Martha.
I await you
as we all await her
fearing her honesty
fearing
we may neither love nor dismiss
Martha with the dross burned away
fearing
condemnation from the essential.

You cannot get closer to death than this Martha
the nearest you've come to living yourself.

Memorial I

If you come as softly
as wind within the trees
you may hear what I hear
see what sorrow sees.

If you come as lightly
as the threading dew
I shall take you gladly
nor ask more of you.

You may sit beside me
silent as a breath
and only those who stay dead
shall remember death.

If you come I will be silent
nor speak harsh words to you—
I will not ask you why, now,
nor how, nor what you knew.

But we shall sit here softly
beneath two different years
and the rich earth between us
shall drink our tears.

Memorial II

Genevieve
what are you seeing
in my mirror this morning
peering out from behind my eyes
like a hungry bird
Are you seeking the shape of a girl
I have grown less and less
to resemble
or do you remember
I could not accept your face dying
I do not know you now
But surely your vision stayed
stronger than mine
Genevieve tell me
where do the dead girls wander
after their summer?

I wish I could see you again
far from me even
birdlike
flying into the sun
your eyes
blind me Genevieve.

The Songless Lark

Sun shines so brightly on the hill
that I can see each day
patches of snow that fell this spring
before you went away.

And now that summer's near at hand
below the meadow springs
behind the trees at dawnlight
a songless lark now sings.

Anniversary

The bitter tears are stone
but one quick breath
remembers love
and the long years you've lain
bride to the thunder
sister to fallen rain
who ate a bitter fruit
to dance with death.

We have no right to love
now you are dead
who could not hold you here.
Our tears
water an alien grass.
All has been said
and you have walked in silence
many years.

But April came today.
though spring comes ever
even in the empty years
since you have slept
it was in April
that you chose to sever
young love and self
and I remembered
and I wept.

Second Spring

We have no passions left to love the spring
who have suffered autumn as we did, alone
walking through dominions of a browning laughter
carrying our loneliness, our loving and our pain.

How shall we know another spring
For there will come no flower where was fruit before
and we have little use for spring's relentless seeking
who walked the long, unquestioned path
straight into autumn's trailing arms
who saw the summer passions wither
into dry leaves to hide our naked tears.

Autumn teaches bearing
and new sun will warm our proud and cautious feet
but spring came once
and we have seen the road that led through summer
beautiful and bright as clover on a hill
become a vast appalling wilderness and rain
while we stood still
racked on the autumn's weeping
binding cold love to us
with the corners of her shroud.

To a Girl Who Knew What Side Her Bread Was Buttered On

He, through the eyes of the first marauder
saw her, his catch of bright thunder, heaping
tea and bread for her guardian dead
crunching the nut-dry words they said
and, thinking the bones were sleeping.
he broke through the muffled afternoon
calling an end to their ritual's tune
with lightning-like disorder:

'Leave these bones, Love! Come away
from their summer breads with the flavour of hay—
your guards can watch the shards of our catch
warming *our* bones on some winter's day!'

Like an ocean of straws the old bones rose up
Fearing his threat of a second death;
and he had little time to wonder
at the silence of bright thunder
as, with a smile of pity and stealth,
she buttered fresh scones for her guardian bones
and they trampled him into the earth.

BETWEEN OUR SELVES

(1976)

for Frances

for the embattled
there is no place
that cannot be
home.
nor is.

Power

The difference between poetry and rhetoric
is being ready to kill
yourself
instead of your children.

I am trapped on a desert of raw gunshot wounds
and a dead child dragging his shattered black
face off the edge of my sleep
blood from his punctured cheeks and shoulders
is the only liquid for miles
and my stomach
churns at the imagined taste while
my mouth splits into dry lips
without loyalty or reason
thirsting for the wetness of his blood
as it sinks into the whiteness
of the desert where I am lost
without imagery or magic
trying to make power out of hatred and destruction
trying to heal my dying son with kisses
only the sun will bleach his bones quicker.

A policeman who shot down a ten year old in Queens
stood over the boy with his cop shoes in childish blood
and a voice said "Die you little motherfucker" and
there are tapes to prove it. At his trial
this policeman said in his own defense
"I didn't notice the size nor nothing else
only the color". And
there are tapes to prove that, too.

Today that 37 year old white man
with 13 years of police forcing
was set free
by eleven white men who said they were satisfied
justice had been done
and one Black Woman who said
"They convinced me" meaning

they had dragged her 4'10" Black Woman's frame
over the hot coals
of four centuries of white male approval
until she let go
the first real power she ever had
and lined her own womb with cement
to make a graveyard for our children.

I have not been able to touch the destruction
within me.
But unless I learn to use
the difference between poetry and rhetoric
my power too will run corrupt as poisonous mold
or lie limp and useless as an unconnected wire
and one day I will take my teenaged plug
and connect it to the nearest socket
raping an 85 year old white woman
who is somebody's mother
and as I beat her senseless and set a torch to her bed
a greek chorus will be singing in 3/4 time
"Poor thing. She never hurt a soul. What beasts they are."

School Note

My children play with skulls
for their classrooms
are guarded by warlocks
who scream at the walls collapsing
into paper toilets
plump witchs mouth ancient curses
in an untaught tongue
test children upon their meanings
assign grades
in a holocaust
ranging
from fury down through contempt.

My children play with skulls
at school
they have already learned
to dream of dying
their playgrounds
were graveyards
where nightmares of no
stood watch over rented earth
filled with the bones of tomorrow.

My children play with skulls
and remember
for the embattled
there is no place
that cannot be
home
nor is.

Solstice

We forgot to water the plantain shoots
when our houses were full of borrowed meat
and our stomachs with the gift of strangers
who laugh now as they pass us
because our land is barren
the farms are choked
with stunted rows of straw
and with our nightmares of juicy brown yams
that cannot fill us.
The roofs of our houses rot from last winter's water
but our drinking pots are broken
we have used them to mourn the death of old lovers
the next rain will wash our footprints away
and our children have married beneath them.

Our skins are empty.
They have been vacated by the spirits
who are angered by our reluctance
to feed them
in baskets of straw made from sleep grass
and the droppings of civets
they have been hidden away by our mothers
who are waiting for us at the river.

My skin is tightening
soon I shall shed it
like a monitor lizard
like remembered comfort
at the new moons rising
I will eat the last signs of my weakness
remove the scars of old childhood wars
and dare to enter the forest whistling
like a snake that had fed the chameleon
for changes
I shall be forever.

May I never remember reasons
for my spirit's safety

may I never forget
the warning of my woman's flesh
weeping at the new moon
may I never lose
that terror
which keeps me brave
may I owe nothing
that I cannot repay.

Scar

This is a simple poem.
For the mothers sisters daughters
girls I have never been
for the women who clean the Staten Island Ferry
for the sleek witches who burn
me at midnight
in effigy
because I eat at their tables
and sleep with their ghosts.

These stones in my heart are you
of my own flesh
whittling me with your sharp false eyes
searching for prisms
falling out of your head
laughing me out of your skin
because you do not value your own
self
nor me.

This is a simple poem
I will have no mother no sister no daughter
when I am through
and only the bones are left
see how the bones are showing
the shape of us at war
clawing our own flesh out
to feed the backside of our masklike faces
that we have given the names of men.

Donald DeFreeze I never knew you so well
as in the eyes of my own mirror
did you hope
for blessing or pardon
lying
in bed after bed
or was your eye sharp and merciless enough

to endure
beyond the deaths of wanting?

With your voice in my ears
with my voice in your ears
try to deny me
I will hunt you down
through the night veins of my own addiction
through all my unsatisfied childhoods
as this poem unfolds
like the leaves of a poppy
I have no sister no mother no children
left
only a tideless ocean of moonlit women
in all shades of loving
learning a dance of open and closing
learning a dance of electrical tenderness
no father no mother would teach them.

Come Sambo dance with me
pay the piper dangling dancing
his knee high darling
over your wanting
under your bloody
white faces come Bimbo come Ding Dong
watch the city falling down down
down lie down bitch slow down nigger
so you want a cozy womb to hide you
to pucker up and suck you back
safely
well I tell you what I'm gonna do
next time you head for the hatchet
really need some nook to hole up in
look me up
I'm the ticket taker on a queen
of rollercoasters
I can get you off
cheap.

This is a simple poem
sharing my head with the dream
of a big black woman with jewels
in her eyes
she dances
her head in a golden helmet
arrogant
plumed
her name is Colossa
her thighs are like stanchions
or flayed hickory trees
embraced in armour
she dances
in slow earth shaking motions
that suddenly alter
and lighten
as she whirls laughing
tooled metal over her hips
comes to an end
and at the shiny edge
an astonishment
of soft black curly hair.

Between Ourselves

Once when I walked into a room
my eyes would seek out the one or two black faces
for contact or reassurance or a sign
I was not alone
now walking into rooms full of black faces
that would destroy me for any difference
where shall my eyes look?
Once it was easy to know
who were my people.

If we were stripped of all pretense
to our strength
and our flesh was cut away
the sun would bleach all our bones
as white
as the face of my black mother
was bleached white by gold
or Orishala
and how
does that measure me?

I do not believe
our wants have made all our lies
holy.

Under the sun on the shores of Elmina
a black man sold the woman who carried
my grandmother in her belly
he was paid with bright yellow coins
that shone in the evening sun
and in the faces of her sons and daughters.
When I see that brother behind my eyes
his irises are bloodless and without colour
his tongue clicks like yellow coins
tossed up on this shore
where we share the same corner
of an alien and corrupted heaven

and whenever I try to eat
the words
of easy blackness as salvation
I taste the colour
of my grandmother's first betrayal.

I do not believe
our wants
have made all our lies
holy.

But I do not whistle this man's name
at the shrine of Shopona
I cannot bring down the rosy juices of death upon him
nor forget Orishala
is called the god of whiteness
who works in the dark wombs of night
forming the shapes we all wear
so that even cripples and dwarfs and albinos
are sacred worshippers
when the boiled corn is offered.

Humility lies
in the face of history
and I have forgiven myself
for him
for the white meat
we all consumed in secret
before we were born
we shared the same meal.
When you impale me
upon your lances of narrow blackness
before you hear my heart speak
mourn your own borrowed blood
your own borrowed visions
singing through a foreign tongue.
Do not mistake my flesh
for the enemy
do not write my name in the dust
before the shrine of the god of smallpox

for we are all children of Eshu
god of chance and the unpredictable
and we each wear many changes
inside of our skin.

Armed with scars
healed
in many different colours
I look into my own faces
as Eshu's daughter
crying
if we do not stop killing
the other
in ourselves
the self that we hate
in others
soon we shall all lie
in the same direction
and Eshidale's priests will be very busy
they who alone can bury
all those who seek their own death
by jumping up from the ground
and landing upon their heads.

Outside

In the center of a harsh and spectrumed city
all things natural are strange.
I grew up in a genuine confusion
between grass and weeds and flowers
and what coloured meant
except for clothes you couldn't bleach
and nobody called me nigger
until I was thirteen.
Nobody lynched my momma
but what she'd never been
had bleached her face of everything
but very private furies
and made the other children
call me yellow snot at school.
And how many times have I called myself back
through my bones confusion
black
like marrow meaning meat
for my soul's hunger
and how many times have you cut me
and run in the streets
my own blood
who do you think me to be
that you are terrified of becoming
or what do you see in my face
you have not already discarded
in your own mirror
what face do you see in my eyes
that you will someday
come to
acknowledge your own?

Who shall I curse that I grew up
believing in my mother's face
or that I lived in fear of the potent darkness
that wore my father's shape
they have both marked me

with their blind and terrible love
and I am lustful now for my own name.

Between the canyons of my parent's silences
mother bright and father brown
I seek my own shapes now
for they never spoke of me
except as theirs
and the pieces that I stumble and fall over
I still record as proof
that I am beautiful
twice
blessed with the images
of who they were
and who I thought them once
to be
of what I move
toward and through
and what I need
to leave behind me
for most of all I am
blessed within my selves
who are come to make our shattered faces
whole.

A Woman/Dirge
for Wasted Children

for Clifford

Awakening
rumours of the necessity for your death
are spread by persistent screaming flickers
in the morning light
I lie
knowing it is past time for sacrifice
and I burn
like the hungry tongue of an ochre fire
like a benediction of fury
pushed before the heel of the hand
of the thunder goddess
parting earth's folds with a searching finger
I yield
one drop of blood
which I know instantly
is lost.

A man has had himself
appointed
legal guardian of fetuses.
Centuries of wasted children
warred and whored and slaughtered
anoint me guardian
for life.

But in the early light
another sacrifice is taken
unchallenged
a small dark shape rolls down
a hilly slope
dragging its trail of wasted blood
onto the ground
I am broken
into clefts of screaming
that sound like the drilling flickers

in treacherous morning air
on murderous sidewalks
I am bent
forever
wiping up blood
that should be
you.

THE BLACK UNICORN

(1978)

For
Linda Gertrude Belmar Lorde

and
Frederick Byron Lorde

The Face Has Many Seasons

The Black Unicorn

The black unicorn is greedy.
The black unicorn is impatient.
The black unicorn was mistaken
for a shadow
or symbol
and taken
through a cold country
where mist painted mockeries
of my fury.
It is not on her lap where the horn rests
but deep in her moonpit
growing.

The black unicorn is restless
the black unicorn is unrelenting
the black unicorn is not
free.

A Woman Speaks

Moon marked and touched by sun
my magic is unwritten
but when the sea turns back
it will leave my shape behind.
I seek no favor
untouched by blood
unrelenting as the curse of love
permanent as my errors
or my pride
I do not mix
love with pity
nor hate with scorn
and if you would know me
look into the entrails of Uranus
where the restless oceans pound.

I do not dwell
within my birth nor my divinities
who am ageless and half-grown
and still seeking
my sisters
witches in Dahomey
wear me inside their coiled cloths
as our mother did
mourning.

I have been woman
for a long time
beware my smile
I am treacherous with old magic
and the noon's new fury
with all your wide futures
promised
I am
woman
and not white.

From the House of Yemanjá

My mother had two faces and a frying pot
where she cooked up her daughters
into girls
before she fixed our dinner.
My mother had two faces
and a broken pot
where she hid out a perfect daughter
who was not me
I am the sun and moon and forever hungry
for her eyes.

I bear two women upon my back
one dark and rich and hidden
in the ivory hungers of the other
mother
pale as a witch
yet steady and familiar
brings me bread and terror
in my sleep
her breasts are huge exciting anchors
in the midnight storm.

All this has been
before
in my mother's bed
time has no sense
I have no brothers
and my sisters are cruel.

Mother I need
mother I need
mother I need your blackness now
as the august earth needs rain.
I am

the sun and moon and forever hungry
the sharpened edge
where day and night shall meet
and not be
one.

Coniagui Women

The Coniagui women
wear their flesh like war
bear children who have eight days
to choose their mothers
it is up to the children
who must decide to stay.

Boys burst from the raised loins
twisting and shouting
from the bush secret
they run
beating the other women
avoiding the sweet flesh
hidden
near their mother's fire
but they must take her blood as a token
the wild trees have warned them
beat her and you will be free
on the third day
they creep up to her cooking pot
bubbling over the evening's fire
and she feeds them
yam soup
and silence.

"Let us sleep in your bed" they whisper
"Let us sleep in your bed" they whisper
"Let us sleep in your bed"
but she has mothered before them.
She closes her door.

They become men.

A Rock Thrown into the Water
Does Not Fear the Cold

In front of the City Hotel in Kumasi
two horned snails come at twilight
to eat the foot-long speckled snake
dead on an evening wall
from sudden violent storm.
Their white extended bodies
gently sucking
take sweetness from the stiffening shape
as darkness overtakes them.

Dahomey

"in spite of the fire's heat
the tongs can fetch it."

It was in Abomey that I felt
the full blood of my fathers' wars
and where I found my mother
Seboulisa
standing with outstretched palms hip high
one breast eaten away by worms of sorrow
magic stones resting upon her fingers
dry as a cough.

In the dooryard of the brass workers
four women joined together dying cloth
mock Eshu's iron quiver
standing erect and flamingly familiar
in their dooryard
mute as a porcupine in a forest of lead
In the courtyard of the cloth workers
other brothers and nephews
are stitching bright tapestries
into tales of blood.

Thunder is a woman with braided hair
spelling the fas of Shango
asleep between sacred pythons
that cannot read
nor eat the ritual offerings
of the Asein.
My throat in the panther's lair
is unresisting.

Bearing two drums on my head I speak
whatever language is needed
to sharpen the knives of my tongue
the snake is aware although sleeping
under my blood

since I am a woman whether or not
you are against me
I will braid my hair
even
in the seasons of rain.

125th Street and Abomey

Head bent, walking through snow
I see you Seboulisa
printed inside the back of my head
like marks of the newly wrapped akai
that kept my sleep fruitful in Dahomey
and I poured on the red earth in your honor
those ancient parts of me
most precious and least needed
my well-guarded past
the energy-eating secrets
I surrender to you as libation
mother, illuminate my offering
of old victories
over men over women over my selves
who has never before dared
to whistle into the night
take my fear of being alone
like my warrior sisters
who rode in defense of your queendom
disguised and apart
give me the woman strength
of tongue in this cold season.

Half earth and time splits us apart
like struck rock.
A piece lives elegant stories
too simply put
while a dream on the edge of summer
of brown rain in nim trees
snail shells from the dooryard
of King Toffah
bring me where my blood moves
Seboulisa mother goddess with one breast
eaten away by worms of sorrow and loss
see me now
your severed daughter
laughing our name into echo
all the world shall remember.

The Women of Dan Dance with Swords in Their Hands to Mark the Time When They Were Warriors

I did not fall from the sky
I
nor descend like a plague of locusts
to drink color and strength from the earth
and I do not come like rain
as a tribute or symbol for earth's becoming
I come as a woman
dark and open
some times I fall like night
softly
and terrible
only when I must die
in order to rise again.

I do not come like a secret warrior
with an unsheathed sword in my mouth
hidden behind my tongue
slicing my throat to ribbons
of service with a smile
while the blood runs
down and out
through holes in the two sacred mounds
on my chest.

I come like a woman
who I am
spreading out through nights
laughter and promise
and dark heat
warming whatever I touch
that is living
consuming
only
what is already dead.

Sahara

High
above this desert
I am
becoming
absorbed.

Plateaus of sand
dendrites of sand
continents and islands and waddys
of sand
tongue sand
wrinkle sand
mountain sand
coasts of sand
pimples and pustules and macula of sand
snot all over your face from sneezing sand
dry lakes of sand
buried pools of sand
moon craters of sand
Get your "I've had too much of people"
out of here sand.

My own place sand
never another place sand
punishments of sand
hosannahs of sand
Epiphanies of sand
crevasses of sand
mother of sand
I've been here a long time sand
string sand
spaghetti sand
cat's cradle ring-a-levio sand
army of trees sand
jungle of sand
grief of sand
subterranean treasure sand

moonglade sand
male sand
terrifying sand

Will I never get out of here sand
open and closed sand
curvatures of sand
nipples of sand
hard erected bosoms of sand
clouds quick and heavy and
desperate sand
thick veil over my face sand
sun is my lover sand
footprints of the time on sand
navel sand
elbow sand
play hopscotch through the labyrinth sand
I have spread myself sand
I have grown harsh and flat
against you sand
glass sand
fire sand
malachite and gold diamond sand
cloisonné coal sand
filagree silver sand
granite and marble and ivory sand

Hey you come here and she came sand
I will endure sand
I will resist sand
I am tired of no
all the time sand
I too will unmask my dark
hard rock sand.

Harriet

Harriet there was always somebody calling us crazy
or mean or stuck-up or evil or black
or black
and we were
nappy girls quick as cuttlefish
scurrying for cover
trying to speak trying to speak
trying to speak
the pain in each others mouths
until we learned
on the edge of a lash
or a tongue
on the edge of the other's betrayal
that respect
meant keeping our distance
in silence
averting our eyes
from each other's face in the street
from the beautiful dark mouth
and cautious familiar eyes
passing alone.

I remember you Harriet
before we were broken apart
we dreamed the crossed swords
of warnor queens
while we avoided each other's eyes
and we learned to know lonely
as the earth learns to know dead
Harriet Harriet
what name shall we call our selves now
our mother is gone?

Chain

News item: Two girls, fifteen and sixteen, were sent to foster
homes, because they had borne children by their natural father.
Later, they petitioned the New York courts to be returned to their
parents, who, the girls said, loved them. And the courts did so.

Faces surround me that have no smell or color no time
only strange laughing testaments
vomiting promise like love
but look at the skeleton children
advancing against us
beneath their faces there is no sunlight
no darkness
no heart remains
no legends
to bring them back as women
into their bodies at dawn.

Look at the skeleton children
advancing against us
we will find womanhood
in their eyes
as they cry
which of you bore me
will love me
will claim my blindness as yours
and which of you marches to battle
from between my legs?

            II
On the porch outside my door
girls are lying
like felled maples in the path of my feet
I cannot step past them nor over them
their slim bodies roll like smooth tree trunks
repeating themselves over and over
until my porch is covered with the bodies
of young girls.
Some have a child in their arms.

To what death shall I look for comfort?
Which mirror to break or mourn?

Two girls repeat themselves in my doorway
their eyes are not stone.
Their flesh is not wood nor steel
but I can not touch them.
Shall I warn them of night
or offer them bread
or a song?
They are sisters. Their father has known
them over and over. The twins they carry
are his. Whose death shall we mourn
in the forest
unburied?
Winter has come and the children are dying.

One begs me to hold her between my breasts
Oh write me a poem mother
here, over my flesh
get your words upon me
as he got this child upon me
our father lover
thief in the night
do not be so angry with us. We told him
your bed was wider
but he said if we did it then
we would be his
good children if we did it
then he would love us
oh make us a poem mother
that will tell us his name
in your language
is he father or lover
we will leave your word
for our children
engraved on a whip or a golden scissors
to tell them the lies
of their birth.

Another says mother
I am holding your place.
Do you know me better than I knew him
or myself?
Am I his daughter or girlfriend
am I your child or your rival
you wish to be gone from his bed?
Here is your granddaughter mother
give us your blessing before I sleep
what other secrets
do you have to tell me
how do I learn to love her
as you have loved me?

Sequelae

Because a burning sword notches both of my doorposts
because I am standing between
my burned hands in the ashprint of two different houses
midnight finds weave a filigree of disorder
I figure in the dreams of people
who do not even know me
the night is a blister of stars
pierced by nightmares of a telephone ringing
my hand is the receiver
threatening as an uncaged motor
seductive as the pain of voiceless mornings
voiceless kitchens I remember
cornflakes shrieking like banshees in my throat
while I battle the shapes of you
wearing old ghosts of me
hating you for being
black and not woman
hating you for being white
and not me
in this carnival of memories
I name you both the laying down of power
the separation I cannot yet make
after all these years of blood
my eyes are glued
like fury to the keyholes
of yesterday
rooms
where I wander
solitary as a hunting cheetah
at play with legends call disaster
due all women who refuse to wait
in vain;

In a new room
I enter old places bearing your shape
trapped behind the sharp smell of your anger

in my voice
behind tempting invitations
to believe
your face
tipped like a pudding under glass
and I hear the high pitch of your voice
crawling out from my hearts
deepest culverts
compromise is a coffin nail
rusty as seaweed
tiding through an august house
where nobody lives
beyond choice
my pathways are strewn with old discontents
outgrown defenses still sturdy as firebrick
unlovely and dangerous as measles
they wither into uselessness
but do not decay.

Because I do not wish
to remember
but love to caress the deepest bone
of me
begging shes that wax and wane like moonfire
to absolve me at any price
I battle old ghosts of you
wearing the shapes of me
surrounded by black
and white faces
saying no over and over
becoming my mother draped in my fathers
bastard ambition
growing dark secrets
out from between her thighs
and night comes into me like a fever
my hands grip a flaming sword that screams
while an arrogant woman masquerading as a fish
plunges it deeper and deeper
into the heart we both share

like beggars
on this moment of time
where the space ships land
I have died too many deaths
that were not mine.

For Assata

New Brunswick Prison, 1977

In this new picture your smile has been to war
you are almost obscured by other faces
on the pages
those shadows are sisters
who have not yet spoken
your face is in shadow
obscured by the half-dark
by the thick bars running across your eyes
like sentinels
all the baby fat has been burned away
like a luxury your body let go
reluctantly
the corners of your mouth turn down
I cannot look into your eyes
who are all those others
behind you
the shadows are growing lighter
and more confusing.

I dream of your freedom
as my victory
and the victory of all dark women
who forego the vanities of silence
who war and weep
sometimes against our selves
in each other
rather than our enemies
falsehoods
Assata my sister warrior
Joan of Arc and Yaa Asantewa
embrace
at the back of your cell.

At First I Thought
You Were Talking About . . .

Do you think I guess inasmuch as
so so
to be sure yes I see
what'd you mean
but listen yet and still on the other
hand like as if you know
oh
at first
I thought you were talking about
a bird a flower
your anguish
the precision of trial by fury
apes in the roses
a body-sized box
even my own mother's sadness
freezing into diamonds
sanctified beyond description
and brilliant as death.

There are 237 footfalls
from the parking lot
to this metal table
this mechanical desk of judgment
the early spring sun
shines
on the face of building
but is cut off at the door
now take my body and blood
as the last recorded sacrifice
of a negative image
upon the revolving doorpane
of this building
where even the elevators are tired

To be sure yes I know what did
you mean by the way

but listen yet and still on the other hand
like you know just as if
do you think I guess in as much as so-so
oh well I see
at first I thought you were talking
about . . .

A Litany for Survival

For those of us who live at the shoreline
standing upon the constant edges of decision
crucial and alone
for those of us who cannot indulge
the passing dreams of choice
who love in doorways coming and going
in the hours between dawns
looking inward and outward
at once before and after
seeking a now that can breed
futures
like bread in our children's mouths
so their dreams will not reflect
the death of ours;

For those of us
who were imprinted with fear
like a faint line in the center of our foreheads
learning to be afraid with our mother's milk
for by this weapon
this illusion of some safety to be found
the heavy-footed hoped to silence us
For all of us
this instant and this triumph
We were never meant to survive.

And when the sun rises we are afraid
it might not remain
when the sun sets we are afraid
it might not rise in the morning
when our stomachs are full we are afraid
of indigestion
when our stomachs are empty we are afraid
we may never eat again
when we are loved we are afraid
love will vanish
when we are alone we are afraid

love will never return
and when we speak we are afraid
our words will not be heard
nor welcomed
but when we are silent
we are still afraid.

So it is better to speak
remembering
we were never meant to survive.

Meet

Woman when we met on the solstice
high over halfway between your world and mine
rimmed with full moon and no more excuses
your red hair burned my fingers as I spread you
tasting your ruff down to sweetness
and I forgot to tell you
I have heard you calling across this land
in my blood before meeting
and I greet you again
on the beaches in mines lying on platforms
in trees full of tail-tail birds flicking
and deep in your caverns of decomposed granite
even over my own laterite hills
after a long journey
licking your sons
while you wrinkle your nose at the stench.

Coming to rest
in the open mirrors of your demanded body
I will be black light as you lie against me
I will be heavy as August over your hair
our rivers flow from the same sea
and I promise to leave you again
full of amazement and our illuminations
dealt through the short tongues of color
or the taste of each other's skin as it hung
from our childhood mouths.

When we meet again
will you put your hands upon me
will I ride you over our lands
will we sleep beneath trees in the rain?
You shall get young as I lick your stomach
hot and at rest before we move off again
you will be white fury in my navel
I will be sweeping night
Mawulisa foretells our bodies
as our hands touch and learn

from each others hurt
Taste my milk in the ditches of Chile and Ouagadougou
in Tema's bright port while the priestess of Larteh
protects us
in the high meat stalls of Palmyra and Abomey-Calavi
now you are my child and my mother
we have always been sisters in pain.

Come in the curve of the lion's bulging stomach
lie for a season out of the judging rain
we have mated we have cubbed
we have high time for work and another meeting
women exchanging blood
in the innermost rooms of moment
we must taste of each other's fruit
at least once
before we shall both be slain.

Seasoning

What am I ready to lose in this advancing summer?
As the days that seemed long
grow shorter and shorter
I want to chew up time
until every moment expands
in an emotional mathematic
that includes the smell and texture
of every similar instant since I was born.

But the solstice is passing
my mouth stumbles
crammed with cribsheets and flowers
dimestore photographs
of loving in stages
choked by flinty nuggets of old friends
undigested enemies
preserved sweet and foul in their lack
of exposure to sunlight.
Thundereggs of myself
ossify in the buttonholes
of old recalled lovers
who all look like rainbows
stretching across other summers
to the pot of gold
behind my own eyes.

As the light wanes
I see
what I thought I was anxious to surrender
I am only willing to lend
and reluctance covers my face
as I glue up my lips with the promise
of coming winter.

Touring

Coming in and out of cities
where I spend one or two days
selling myself
where I spend one or two nights
in beds that do not have the time to fit me
coming in and out of cities
too quickly
to be touched by their magic
I burn
from the beds that do not fit me
I leave sated
but without feeling
any texture of the house I have invaded
by invitation
I leave
with a disturbing sense
of the hard core of flesh
missed
and truly revealing.

I leave poems behind me
dropping them like dark seeds that
I will never harvest
that I will never mourn
if they are destroyed
they pay for a gift
I have not accepted.

Coming in and out of cities
untouched by their magic
I think without feeling
this is what men do
who try for some connection
and fail
and leave
five dollars on the table.

Walking Our Boundaries

This first bright day has broken
the back of winter.
We rise from war
to walk across the earth
around our house
both stunned that sun can shine so brightly
after all our pain
Cautiously we inspect our joint holding.
A part of last year's garden still stands
bracken
one tough missed okra pod clings to the vine
a parody of fruit cold-hard and swollen
underfoot
one rotting shingle
is becoming loam.

I take your hand beside the compost heap
glad to be alive and still
with you
we talk of ordinary articles
with relief
while we peer upward
each half-afraid
there will be no tight buds started
on our ancient apple tree
so badly damaged by last winter's storm
knowing
it does not pay to cherish symbols
when the substance
lies so close at hand
waiting to be held
your hand
falls off the apple bark
like casual fire
along my back
my shoulders are dead leaves
waiting to be burned
to life.

The sun is watery warm
our voices
seem too loud for this small yard
too tentative for women
so in love
the siding has come loose in spots
our footsteps hold this place
together
as our place
our joint decisions make the possible
whole
I do not know when
we shall laugh again
but next week
we will spade up another plot
for this spring's seeding.

Eulogy for Alvin Frost

I

Black men bleeding to death inside themselves
inside their fine strong bodies
inside their stomachs
inside their heads
a hole
as large as a dum-dum bullet
eaten away from the inside
death at 37.

Windows are holes to let in the light
in Newark airport at dawn I read
of your death by illumination
the carpets are dark and the windows are smoky
to keep out the coming sun
I plummet down through a hole in the carpet
seeking immediate ground for my feet to embrace
my toes have no wisdom no strength
to resist
they curl in a spasm of grief
of fury uprooted
It is dawn in the airport and nothing is open
I cannot even plant you a tree
the earth is still frozen
I write a card saying
machines grew the flowers I send
to throw into your grave.

On occasion we passed in the hallway
usually silent and hurried but fighting
on the same side.
You congratulate me on my latest book
in a Black Caucus meeting
you are distinguished
by your genuine laughter
and you might have been my long lost
second grade seat-mate named Alvin

grown into some other magic
but we never had time enough
just to talk.

II

From an airplane heading south
the earth grows slowly greener
we pass the first swimming pool
filled with blue water
this winter is almost over
I don't want to write a natural poem
I want to write about the unnatural death
of a young man at 37
eating himself for courage in secret
until he vanished
bleeding to death inside.
He will be eulogized in echoes
by a ghost of those winters
that haunt morning people
wearing away our days like smiling water
in southern pools
leaving psychic graffiti
clogging the walls of our hearts
carving out ulcers inside our stomachs
from which we explode
or bleed to death.

III

The day after your burial
John Wade slid off his chair
onto the carpet in the student cafeteria
and died there on the floor
between Abnormal Psychology and a half-finished
cup of black coffee.
Cafeteria guards rushed him out
the back door between classes
and we never knew until a week later
that he had even been ill.

I am tired of writing memorials to black men
whom I was on the brink of knowing
weary like fig trees
weighted like a crepe myrtle
with all the black substance poured into earth
before earth is ready to bear.
I am tired of holy deaths
of the ulcerous illuminations the cerebral accidents
the psychology of the oppressed
where mental health is the ability
to repress
knowledge of the world's cruelty.

IV
Dear Danny who does not know me
I am
writing to you for your father
whom I barely knew
except at meetings where he was
distinguished
by his genuine laughter
and his kind bright words
Danny son of Alvin
please cry
whenever it hurts
remember to laugh
even when you do battle
stay away from coffee and fried plastic
even when it looks like chicken
and grow up
black and strong and beautiful
but not too soon.

We need you
and there are so few
left.

Chorus

Sun
make me whole again
to love
the shattered truths of me
spilling out like dragon's teeth
through the hot lies
of those who say they love
me
when I am done
each shard will spring up
complete and armed
like a warrior woman
hot to be dealt with
slipping through alleyways
of musical night people humming
Mozart
was a white dude.

Coping

It has rained for five days
running
the world is
a round puddle
of sunless water
where small islands
are only beginning
to cope
a young boy
in my garden
is bailing out water
from his flower patch
when I ask him why
he tells me
young seeds that have not seen sun
forget
and drown easily.

To Martha: A New Year

As you search over this year
with eyes your heart has
sharpened
remember longing.

I do not know your space now
I only seek a woman whom I love
trapped there
by accident.
but places do not change
so much
as what we seek in them
and faith will serve
along the way
to somewhere else
where work begins.

In Margaret's Garden

When I first saw you blooming the color was now
protests sprang from your rapid hands
like a second set of fingers
you were learning to use
the betrayal of others
in place of your own pain
and your mouth was smiling
off-center
in the total confusion.

I never saw nor visited by day
the place where your swans
were conquered.
When I met you again
your mouth had centered
into aloneness
you said you had come apart
but your earth had been nourished
into a new garden of strong smells.

I felt you wanting
to mourn
the innocence of beginnings
that old desire for blandness.
I feel your sadness
deep in the center of me
and I make a pact with you sister
if you will not sorrow
I will not tell.

Scar

This is a simple poem.
for the mothers sisters daughters
girls I have never been
for the women who clean the Staten Island ferry
for the sleek witches who burn
me at midnight
in effigy
because I eat at their tables
and sleep with their ghosts.

Those stones in my heart are you
of my own flesh
whittling me with your sharp false eyes
laughing me out of your skin
because you do not value your own
life
nor me.

This is a simple poem
I will have no mother no sister no daughter
when I am through
and only the bones are left
see how the bones are showing
the shape of us at war
clawing our own flesh out
to feed the backside of our masklike faces
that we have given the names of men.

Donald DeFreeze I never knew you so well
as in the eyes of my own mirror
did you hope
for blessing or pardon
lying
in bed after bed
or was your eye sharp and merciless enough
to endure
beyond the deaths of wanting?

With your voice in my ears
with my voice in your ears
try to deny me
I will hunt you down
through the night veins of my own addiction
through all my unsatisfied childhoods
as this poem unfolds
like the leaves of a poppy
I have no sister no mother no children
left
only a tideless ocean of moonlit women
in all shades of loving
learning the dance of open and closing
learning a dance of electrical tenderness
no father no mother would teach them.

Come Sambo dance with me
pay the piper dangling dancing
his knee-high darling
over your wanting under your bloody
white faces come Bimbo come Ding Dong
watch the city falling down down
down lie down bitch slow down nigger
so you want a cozy womb to hide you
to pucker up and suck you back
safely
well I tell you what I'm gonna do
next time you head for the hatchet
really need some nook to hole up in
look me up
I'm the ticket taker on a queen
of roller coasters
I can get you off
cheap.

This is a simple poem
sharing my head with dreams
of a big black woman with jewels in her eyes
she dances

her head in a golden helmet
arrogant
plumed
her name in Colossa
her thighs are like stanchions
or flayed hickory trees
embraced in armour
she dances
slow earth-shaking motions
that suddenly alter
and lighten
as she whirls laughing
the tooled metal over her hips
comes to an end
and at the shiny edge
an astonishment
of soft black curly hair.

Portrait

Strong women
know the taste
of their own hatred
I must always be
building nests
in a windy place
I want the safety of oblique numbers
that do not include me
a beautiful woman
with ugly moments
secret and patient
as the amused and ponderous elephants
catering to Hannibal's ambition
as they swayed on their own way
home.

A Song for Many Movements

Nobody wants to die on the way
caught between ghosts of whiteness
and the real water
none of us wanted to leave
our bones
on the way to salvation
three planets to the left
a century of light years ago
our spices are separate and particular
but our skins sing in complimentary keys
at a quarter to eight mean time
we were telling the same stories
over and over and over.

Broken down gods survive
in the crevasses and mudpots
of every beleaguered city
where it is obvious
there are too many bodies
to cart to the ovens
or gallows
and our uses have become
more important than our silence
after the fall
too many empty cases
of blood to bury or burn
there will be no body left
to listen
and our labor
has become more important
than our silence.

Our labor has become
more important
than our silence.

Brother Alvin

In the seat that we shared in the second grade
there was always a space between us
left for our guardian angels.
We had made it out of the brownies together
because you knew your numbers
and could find the right pages
while I could read all the words.
You were absent a lot between Halloween
and Thanksgiving
and just before Christmas vacation
you disappeared
along with the tinsel
and paper turkeys
and never returned.

My guardian angel and I had the seat to ourselves
for a little while only
until I was demoted back to the brownies
because I could never find the correct page.

You were not my first death.
but your going was not solaced by the usual
rituals of separation
the dark lugubrious murmurs
and invitations by threat
to the dignified grownups' view
of a child's inelegant pain
so even now
all these years of death later
I search through the index
of each new book
on magic
hoping to find some new spelling
of your name.

School Note

My children play with skulls
for their classrooms are guarded by warlocks
who scream at the walls collapsing
into paper toilets
plump witches mouth ancient curses
in an untaught tongue
test children upon their meaning
assign grades
in a holocaust ranging
from fury down through contempt.

My children play with skulls
at school
they have already learned
to dream of dying
their playgrounds were graveyards
where nightmares of no
stand watch over rented earth
filled with the bones of tomorrow.

My children play with skulls
and remember
for the embattled
there is no place
that cannot be
home
nor is.

Digging

In the rusty pages of Gray's Anatomy
in witchcraft and chewing gum
on sundays
I have sought you in the rings around oak trees
on each of the twelve moons of Jupiter
on Harlem streets
peeping up at the secrets pregnant women carry
like a swollen threat
beneath the flowers of their gathered blouses
and under the breasts of a summer night
smelling of the kerosene and red pepper
my mother used to frighten out bedbugs
hidden between my toes
or was it only dream beads of sweat
I suffered
before I could slip
through nightmare
into the patient world of sleep
vanishing like a swallowed flower
and for years afterward I would wake
in August
to the left-over scent
of a child's tears
on my pillow.

In the stone machine
that smells of malachite and jasper
of coprolites undercutting and crazed
in the stone machine
twirled green dust burns my nose
like Whitsuntide fire.

I send you a gift of Malachite.
Of Amber, for melancholy.
Of Turquoise, for your heart's ease.

In the stone museum
ancient tapestries
underline sense
with an animal
touching the organ's place.

Outside

In the center of a harsh and spectrumed city
all things natural are strange.
I grew up in a genuine confusion
between grass and weeds and flowers
and what colored meant
except for clothes you couldn't bleach
and nobody called me nigger
until I was thirteen.
Nobody lynched my momma
but what she'd never been
had bleached her face of everything
but very private furies
and made the other children
call me yellow snot at school.

And how many times have I called myself back
through my bones confusion
black
like marrow meaning meat
and how many times have you cut me
and run in the streets
my own blood
who do you think me to be
that you are terrified of becoming
or what do you see in my face
you have not already discarded
in your own mirror
what face do you see in my eyes
that you will someday
come to
acknowledge your own?
Who shall I curse that I grew up
believing in my mother's face
or that I lived in fear of potent darkness
wearing my father's shape
they have both marked me

with their blind and terrible love
and I am lustful now for my own name.

Between the canyons of their mighty silences
mother bright and father brown
I seek my own shapes now
for they never spoke of me
except as theirs
and the pieces I stumble and fall over
I still record as proof
that I am beautiful
twice
blessed with the images
of who they were
and who I thought them once to be
of what I move
toward and through
and what I need
to leave behind me
most of all
I am blessed within my selves
who are come to make our shattered faces
whole.

Therapy

Trying to see you
my eyes grow
confused
it is not your face
they are seeking
fingering through your spaces
like a hungry child
even now
I do not want
to make a poem
I want to make you
more and less
a part
from my self.

The Same Death Over and Over
or
Lullabies Are for Children

"It's the small deaths in the supermarket" she said
trying to open my head
with her meat white cleaver
trying to tell me how
her pain met mine
halfway
between the smoking ruins in a black neighborhood of Los Angeles
and the bloody morning streets of child-killing New York.

Her poem reached like an arc across country and
"I'm trying to hear you" I said
roaring with my pain in a predawn city
where it is open season on black children
where my worst lullaby goes on over and over.
"I'm not fighting you" I said
"but it's the small deaths in the gutter
that are unmaking us all
and the white cop who shot down 10-year-old Clifford Glover
did not fire because he saw a girl."

Ballad for Ashes

Nobody lives!
cried the thin man
high on the sunny stone steps
of my house
dreaming
he lied
I saw him come
flying
down to the ground
with a thud.

I touched his bruised face
with my fingers
in the low sun.

A man crept up
to a golden cup
to beg for a drink
the water was cold
but the edges of gold
slit his lips like a sieve.

A Woman/Dirge
for Wasted Children

for Clifford

Awakening
rumors of the necessity for your death
are spread by persistent screaming flickers
in the morning light
I lie
knowing it is past time for sacrifice
I burn
like the hungry tongue of an ochre fire
like a benediction of fury
pushed before the heel of the hand
of the thunder goddess
parting earth's folds with a searching finger
I yield
one drop of blood
which I know instantly
is lost.

A man has had himself
appointed
legal guardian of fetuses.
Centuries of wasted children
warred and whored and slaughtered
anoint me guardian
for life.

But in the early light
another sacrifice is taken
unchallenged
a small dark shape rolls down
a hilly slope
dragging its trail of wasted blood
upon the ground
I am broken
into clefts of screaming

that sound like the drilling flickers
in treacherous morning air
on murderous sidewalks
I am bent
forever
wiping up blood
that should be
you.

Parting

Belligerent and beautiful as a trapped ibis
your lean hands are a sacrifice
spoken three times
before dawn
there is blood in the morning egg
that makes me turn and weep
I see you
weaving pain into garlands
the shape of a noose
while I grow
weary
of licking my heart
for moisture
cactus tongued.

Timepiece

In other destinies of choice
you could have come redheaded
with a star between your thighs
and morning like tender mushrooms
rising up around your toes
curled like a Shantung woman's toes
pausing to be loved
in the rice fields at noon
or as sharpened young eyeteeth
guarded in elegant blackness
erotic and hidden as yam shoots
in the parted mouth of dawn
balancing your craft as we went
upstream for water
Elegba's clay pot whistling upon your head.

But we were new for this time
and used wild-edged pieces of rock
struck off with a blunted hammer
spread
under high sun
and the rocks cry out
while we tell the course
of each other's tongue
with stones
in the place where the priestess
hurtled out palm-nuts
from enchanted fingers
and the stones mix
the colors of rainbows
flashing
you came like a wheaten song.

Fog Report

In this misty place where hunger finds us
seeking direction
I am too close to you to be useful.
When I speak
the smell of love on my breath
distracts you
and it is easier for me
to move
against myself in you
than to solve my own equations.

I am often misled
by your familiar comforts
the shape of your teeth is written
into my palm like a second lifeline
when I am fingerprinted
the taste of your thighs
shows up
outlined in the ink.
They found me wandering at the edge
of a cliff
beside nightmares of your body
"Give us your name and place of birth
and we will show you the way home."

I am tempted
to take you apart
and reconstruct your orifices
your tongue your truths your fleshy altars
into my own forgotten image
so when this fog lifts
I could be sure to find you
tethered like a goat
in my heart's yard.

Pathways:
From Mother to Mother

Tadpoles are legless and never learn to curtsy
birds cannot pee
in spring
black snakes go crazy
bowing out of the presence of kings.
Digging beneath a river bed
whose heart is black and rosy
I find the sticky ooze I learned
rejecting all my angels.
It puzzled my unborn children
and they paused in my frightened womb
a decade or two long
breaking apart what was begun
as marriage. My mother wept.
Fleshy lemmings dropped like corn
into her hopper
popping as they hit the water
and hungry tadpoles
winnowed up my falls.

Wherever she wore ivory
I wear pain.

Imprisoned in the pews of memory
beneath the scarlet velvet
is a smile. My mother
weeping
gouts of bloody wisdom
pewed oracular and seminal as rape
pursues me through the nightmares
of this wonderland of early learning
where I wander cryptic as a saint
tightmouthed as cuttlefish
darting beneath and over
vital flaws unstitched like crazy patchwork
until analyzed and useless I

crest in a shoal of missing mommies
paid and made in beds of consecration
worshiped by rituals in which
I do not believe
nor find a place to kneel and rest
out of the storm of strangers and demands
drowning in flooded churches
thick with rot and swollen with confusion
lashed to a raft of grins aligned in an enemy reason
I refuse to learn again.

Item birds cannot pee
and so they shat upon our heads
while we learned how
to bow
out
of the presence of kings.

Death Dance for a Poet

Hidden in a forest of questions
unwilling to embrace blackthorn trees
to yield
to go into madness gracefully
or alone
the woman is no longer young
she has come to hate slowly
her skin of transparent metal
the sinuous exposure without reprieve
her eyes of clay
heavy with the fruit of prophetic dreaming.

In the hungers of silence
she has stolen her father's judgments
as the moon kneels
she lies
with her lover sun
wild with the pain
of her meticulous chemistry
her blind answers
the woman is eating her magic alone
crusts of quiet
breed a delusion
she is eternal
and stripping herself of night
she wanders
pretending
a borrowed fire
within her eyes.

Under the myrtle tree
unconcerned with not being
a birch
the woman with skin of transparent metal
lies on a cloak of sleep grass
closing at the first touch
unrelieved

clay-eyed and holy beyond comfort or mercy
she accepts the burden of sun
pouring a pan of burning salt
over her shining body
over the piercing revelations
of sinew and bone
her skin grows
soft and opaque.

And out of the ashes
and her range of vision
the executioners advance.

Dream/Songs from the Moon of Beulah Land I–V

I

How much love can I pour into you I said
before it runs out of you
like undigested spinach
or shall I stuff you
like a ritual goose
with whatever you think
you want of me
and for whose killing
shall I grow you up
to leave me
to mourn
in the broken potsherds
upon my doorstep
in silent tears of the empty morning?

But I'm not going anywhere you said
why is there always
another question
beyond the last question
answered
out of your mouth
another storm?
It's happening
I said.

II

Whenever I look for you the wind
howls with danger
beware the tree arms scream
what you are seeking
will find you
in the night
in the fist of your dreaming
and in my mouth
the words became sabers

cutting my boundaries
to ribbons
of merciless light.

III

I dreamt you were driving me
in a big black Mazda
the car with a rotary engine
that ate up three kinds of gas at the same time
and whenever we came
to a station upon our journey
I would have to jump out
and explain
to the redfaced attendant
with a panting hose in his hand
that each kind of gas
gave us very different mileage
and we needed them all
for the combined use of all three
would get us to where we were going
with a great economy
of energy.

IV

You say I am
sound as a drum
but that's very hard to be
as you cover your ears
with academic parchment
be careful
you might rip the cover
with your sharp nails
and then I will not sound at all.

To put us another way
what I come wrapped in
should be familiar to you
as hate is
what I come wrapped in
is close to you

as love is
close
to death
or your lying tongue
surveying the countries
of our mouths.

If I were drum
you would beat me
listening for the echo
of your own touch

not seeking
the voice of the spirit
inside the drum
only the spreading out shape
of your own hand on my skin
cover.

If I ever really sounded
I would rupture
your eardrums
or your heart.

V
Learning to say goodbye
is finding a new tomorrow
on some cooler planet
barren and unfamiliar
and guiltless.

It costs the journey
to learn
letting go
of the burn-out rockets
to learn how
to light up space
with the quick fire of refusal
then drift gently down
to the dead surface
of the moon.

Recreation

Coming together
it is easier to work
after our bodies
meet
paper and pen
neither care nor profit
whether we write or not
but as your body moves
under my hands
charged and waiting
we cut the leash
you create me against your thighs
hilly with images
moving through our word countries
my body
writes into your flesh
the poem
you make of me.

Touching you I catch midnight
as moon fires set in my throat
I love you flesh into blossom
I made you
and take you made
into me.

Woman

I dream of a place between your breasts
to build my house like a haven
where I plant crops
in your body
an endless harvest
where the commonest rock
is moonstone and ebony opal
giving milk to all of my hungers
and your night comes down upon me
like a nurturing rain.

Timing

In our infancy of action we were women of peace
come to service islands with no bridges in sight
in the beginning we all dreamed of an ending
but the wars of our childhood have aged us.

When donations of soup from my yesterday's kitchen
sour in the stomachs of beggars now miles away
and they toss in their sleep in doorways
with a curse of worry upon their lips
then even my good deeds are suspect
fulfillments of dreams of the dead
printing so many starvations
upon our future.
While we labor to feed the living
beware the spirit of the uneasy dead
who trap us into believing
in the too simple.

Our childhood wars have aged us
but it is the absence of change
which will destroy us
which has crippled our harvest into nightmare
of endless plowing through fields rank with death
while the carcasses of 4 million blackbirds
frozen to death because their chatter
insulted the generals
escape in the back pages
like the three black girls
hauled into an empty hurried courtroom
to point fingers at their mother—
I was cooking peasoup while they murmured—
"Yes, Mommy told us that she'd killed him
in front of many strangers she told us
yes he was a white man, may we go now?"
And their eyes look like old women who sleep
in the curve of neon doorways under newspaper
clutching a can of petfood for tomorrow's meal.

Sisters there is a hole in my heart
that is bearing your shapes
over and over
as I read only the headlines
of this morning's newspaper.

Ghost

Since I don't want to trip over your silence
over the gap that is you
in my dark
I will deal how it feels
with you
climbing another impossible mountain
with you gone
away a long time ago.

I don't want my life to be woven or chosen
from pain I am concealing
from fractions of myself
from your voice crying out in your sleep
to another woman
come play in the snow love
but this is not the same winter.

That was our first season of cold
I counted the patterned snowflakes
of love melting into ice
concealing our dreams of separation
I could not bear to write
our names on the mailbox
I could not bear to tell you my dreams
nor to question yours
now this poem
makes those mornings real again.

"You were always real" Bernice is saying
but I see the scars of her pain
hidden beneath the flesh on her cheekbones
and I do not know how many years I spent
trying to forget you
but I am afraid to think
how many years I will spend
trying to remember.

Artisan

In workshops without light
we have made birds
that do not sing
kites that shine
but cannot fly
with the speed
by which light falls
in the throat
of delicate working fire
I thought I had discovered
a survival kit
buried
in the moon's heart
flat and resilient as turtles
a case of tortoise shell
hung
in the mouth of darkness
precise unlikely markings
carved into the carapace
sweet meat beneath.

I did not recognize
the shape
of my own name.

Our bed spread
is a midnight flower
coming
all the way down
to the floor
there
your craft shows.

Letter for Jan

No I don't think you were chicken not to speak
I think you
afraid I was mama as laser
seeking to eat out or change your substance
Mawulisa bent on destruction by threat
who might cover you
in a thick dark cloud of guilty symbols
smelling of sandalwood and old buffalo musk
of fiery offerings in the new moon's chalice
that would seduce you open
turning erotic and delightful as you
went under for the third time
your own poetry and sweetness
masked and drying out
upon your lips.

I do not even know
who looks like you
of all the sisters who come to me
at nightfall
we touch each other in secret places
draw old signs and stories
upon each other's back and proofread
each other's ancient copy.

You did not come to me speaking
because you feared
me as I might have been
god mother grown affluent
with the payment of old debts
or because you imaged me
as quick chic cutting
your praise song shared
to ribbons
thankless and separate as stormy gulfs
where lightning raged to pierce your clit
with proud black anger

or to reject you back into your doubt
smothering you into acceptance
with my own black song
coming over and over
as angry nightmares upon your pillow
to swallow you into confusion like a cherished berry
or buy you up at random with my electric body
shooting out rhythm and symbol
like lasers to burn you up and vanish
before the night.

When all the time
I would have loved you
speaking
being a woman full of loving
turned on
and a little bit raunchy
and heavy
with my own black song.

Bicentennial Poem # 21,000,000

I know
the boundaries of my nation lie
within myself
but when I see old movies
of the final liberation of Paris
with french tanks rumbling over land
that is their own again
and old french men weeping
hats over their hearts
singing a triumphant national anthem

My eyes fill up with muddy tears
that have no earth to fall upon.

The Old Days

Everyone wants to know
how it was in the old days
with no sun or moon in our colorless sky
to warn us we were not insane
only the harsh searing eye
of unblinking madwomen and men
calling our star a zoo
and I have no bride to recall
only many women who whisper
I was always a virgin
because I never remained.

I remember you only through the eyes
of all the forgotten others
on Monday a cat in the sorceresses' alley
screeched out your death
in another year's language
and I had forgotten
your name
like a promise of hunger.

Everyone wants to know how
it was
in the old days
when we kissed stone into dust
eternally hungry
paying respect to the crippled earth
in silence and in tears
surely one star fell as the mountain
collapsed over our bodies
surely the moon blinked once
as our vigils began.

Contact Lenses

Lacking what they want to see
makes my eyes hungry
and eyes can feel
only pain.

Once I lived behind thick walls
of glass
and my eyes belonged
to a different ethic
timidly rubbing the edges
of whatever turned them on.
Seeing usually
was a matter of what was
in front of my eyes
matching what was
behind my brain.
Now my eyes have become
a part of me exposed
quick risky and open
to all the same dangers.

I see much
better now
and my eyes hurt.

Lightly

Don't make waves
is good advice
from a leaky boat.

One light year is the distance
one ray of light can travel in one year and
thirty
light years away from earth
in our infinitely offended universe
of waiting
an electronic cloud announces our presence
finally
to the unimpressable stars.

This is straight from a Scientific American
on the planet earth
our human signature upon the universe
is an electronic cloud
of expanding 30-year-old television programs
like Howdy Doody Arthur Godfrey
Uncle Miltie and Hulahoops
quiz shows and wrestling midgets
baseball
the McCarthy hearings and Captain Kangaroo.

Now I don't know what
a conscious universe might be
but it is interesting to wonder
what will wave back
to all that.

Hanging Fire

I am fourteen
and my skin has betrayed me
the boy I cannot live without
still sucks his thumb
in secret
how come my knees are
always so ashy
what if I die
before morning
and momma's in the bedroom
with the door closed.

I have to learn how to dance
in time for the next party
my room is too small for me
suppose I die before graduation
they will sing sad melodies
but finally
tell the truth about me
There is nothing I want to do
and too much
that has to be done
and momma's in the bedroom
with the door closed.

Nobody even stops to think
about my side of it
I should have been on Math Team
my marks were better than his
why do I have to be
the one
wearing braces
I have nothing to wear tomorrow
will I live long enough
to grow up
and momma's in the bedroom
with the door closed.

But What Can You Teach My Daughter

What do you mean
no no no no
you don't have the right
to know
how often
have we built each other
as shelters
against the cold
and even my daughter knows
what you know
can hurt you
she says her nos
and it hurts
she says
when she talks of liberation
she means freedom
from that pain
she knows
what you know
can hurt
but what you do
not know
can kill.

From Inside an Empty Purse

Money cannot buy you
what you want
standing flatfooted
and lying
like a grounded chestnut
unlovable and suspect
I am trying to reach
you
on whatever levels
you flow from
treacherous growing
water
in a blind tongueless pond.

I am the thread of your woman's cloth
the sexy prison that protects you
deep and unspoken
flesh around your freedom
I am your enemy's face.

The money doesn't matter
so much
as the lie
telling
you don't know
why
in a dream
I am trying to reach
you before
you fall in
to me.

A Small Slaughter

Day breaks without thanks or caution
past a night without satisfaction or pain.
My words are blind children I have armed
against the casual insolence of morning
without you
I am scarred and marketed
like a streetcorner in Harlem
a woman
whose face in the tiles
your feet have not yet regarded
I am the stream
past which you will never step
the woman you can not deal with
I am the mouth
of your scorn.

From the Greenhouse

Summer rains like my blood cries
lover my lover
over and over surging receding sometimes
a brief sun knifing through
rain like my blood speaks
in alternate whispers
roaring giving and taking seeking destroying
beseeching green sprouts
in our struggling garden
blessing the earth as it suffers
blind rain beating down
tender sprouts
in the silent mud.

My blood yells against
your sleeping shoulder
this is a poem of summer
my blood screams at your false safety
your mute body beside me
driving me closer and closer
you seek your own refuge
farther and farther away
in your dreaming
the edge of our bed is approaching
again
rain surges against our windows
green sprouts are drowning
in mud and blessings
in our carefully planted greenhouse
I have moved as far as I can
now my blood merges
into your dreaming.

Journeystones I–XI

I
Maxine
I used to admire your talent
for saying nothing
so well
that way the blood
was always someone else's
and there was always
someplace left
to be yourself
the stranger.

II
Elaine
my sister outsider
I still salute
the power of learning
loss.

III
China
girl on the run
I am sorry
our night
was not black enough
for you
to hide in.

IV
Jan
was a name
for so many people
I cannot remember
you.

V

Margaret
the broken rock you dropped
into my pocket
had unrelenting curves
that would not polish.
I discovered
it was the petrified half-shell
of a prehistoric nut.

VI

Catherine
you lie
against the earth
like a little pungent onion
and whenever I come
too close to you
I weep.

VII

Isabel
I hear your blood ring
but I am tired
of friends who hurt
and lean
at the same time
my heart grows
confused
between your need for love
and your need for destruction.

VIII

Joyce
you always hated
being furious
and without anyone
to kill.

IX
Janie
I feel the scream
drowning in your sharp eyes
trained to impersonate mermaids
shallow seductive
and dangerous as coral.

X
Flora my sister
what I know
I no longer need
to understand.

If you make me stone
I will bruise you.

XI
The last hole in fortune
is the anger of the empress
knowing herself as mortal
and without child.

About Religion

After church
on Sundays
I learned to love
the gospel music
swelling up past garbage cans in the summer
backyards of my childhood armageddon.

Black shiny women
spicy as rocking pumpkins
encased in stiff white covers
long sleeved
silk against brick
and their rocketed beat
snapped like pea shooters
in the august time
while the fingered tambourines
hand heeled beat
rose through the air shafts
sweet and timely.

I hear the music filtered
through a heat wave
of my mother's churchly disapproval.
A skinny nappy-headed little girl
ran back and forth collecting
in my envy
coins wrapped in newspapers
and the corners of old sheets
that even my mother
grudgingly
flung down.

Sister Outsider

We were born in a poor time
never touching
each other's hunger
never
sharing our crusts
in fear
the bread became enemy.

Now we raise our children
to respect themselves
as well as each other.

Now you have made loneliness
holy and useful
and no longer needed
now
your light shines very brightly
but I want you
to know
your darkness also
rich
and beyond fear.

Bazaar

The lay back women are cooking
gold in their iron pots
is smoking
toward a sky that will never speak
in this evening I hold them
bound in the skin of my mother
anxious and ugly as a lump of iron
wishing to be worked for gold
other forgotten faces
of her
flow into each other
over the clatter
of remembered bargains
reluctant barter
I wonder
how many of these women (my sisters)
still have milk in their breasts.

Power

The difference between poetry and rhetoric
is being
ready to kill
yourself
instead of your children.

I am trapped on a desert of raw gunshot wounds
and a dead child dragging his shattered black
face off the edge of my sleep
blood from his punctured cheeks and shoulders
is the only liquid for miles and my stomach
churns at the imagined taste while
my mouth splits into dry lips
without loyalty or reason
thirsting for the wetness of his blood
as it sinks into the whiteness
of the desert where I am lost
without imagery or magic
trying to make power out of hatred and destruction
trying to heal my dying son with kisses
only the sun will bleach his bones quicker.

The policeman who shot down a 10-year-old in Queens
stood over the boy with his cop shoes in childish blood
and a voice said "Die you little motherfucker" and
there are tapes to prove that. At his trial
this policeman said in his own defense
"I didn't notice the size or nothing else
only the color." and
there are tapes to prove that, too.

Today that 37-year-old white man with 13 years of police forcing
has been set free
by 11 white men who said they were satisfied
justice had been done
and one black woman who said
"They convinced me" meaning

they had dragged her 4′10″ black woman's frame
over the hot coals of four centuries of white male approval
until she let go the first real power she ever had
and lined her own womb with cement
to make a graveyard for our children.

I have not been able to touch the destruction within me.
But unless I learn to use
the difference between poetry and rhetoric
my power too will run corrupt as poisonous mold
or lie limp and useless as an unconnected wire
and one day I will take my teenaged plug
and connect it to the nearest socket
raping an 85-year-old white woman
who is somebody's mother
and as I beat her senseless and set a torch to her bed
a greek chorus will be singing in 3/4 time
"Poor thing. She never hurt a soul. What beasts they are."

Eulogy

A girl in my sister's house
wears nightmare
hidden in her eyes
still as a bird's eyes.
When blood calls
the girl retreats into a brassy ring
that neither tears nor nourishment
can alter.

But a circle does not suffer
nor can it dream.
Her fingers twist into a married root
night cannot break her now
nor the sun heal
and soon its merciless white heat
will fuse
her nightmare eyes
to agate
her sullen tongue
to flint.

Then she will strike
but never bleed again.

"Never Take Fire
from a Woman"

My sister and I
have been raised to hate
genteelly
each other's silences
sear up our tongues
like flame
we greet each other
with respect
meaning
from a watchful distance
while we dream of lying
in the tender of passion
to drink from a woman
who smells like love.

Between Ourselves

Once when I walked into a room
my eyes would seek out the one or two black faces
for contact or reassurance or a sign
I was not alone
now walking into rooms full of black faces
that would destroy me for any difference
where shall my eyes look?
Once it was easy to know
who were my people.

If we were stripped to our strength
of all pretense
and our flesh was cut away
the sun would bleach all our bones as white
as the face of my black mother
was bleached white by gold
or Orishala
and how
does that measure me?

I do not believe
our wants have made all our lies
holy.

Under the sun on the shores of Elmina
a black man sold the woman who carried
my grandmother in her belly
he was paid with bright yellow coin
that shone in the evening sun
and in the faces of her sons and daughters.
When I see that brother behind my eyes
his irises are bloodless and without color
his tongue clicks like yellow coins
tossed up on this shore
where we share the same corner
of an alien and corrupted heaven
and whenever I try to eat

the words
of easy blackness as salvation
I taste the color
of my grandmother's first betrayal.

I do not believe
our wants
have made all our lies
holy.

But I do not whistle his name at the shrine of Shopona
I do not bring down the rosy juices of death upon him
nor forget Orishala
is called the god of whiteness
who works in the dark wombs of night
forming the shapes we all wear
so that even cripples and dwarfs and albinos
are scared worshipers
when the boiled corn is offered.

Humility lies
in the face of history
I have forgiven myself
for him
for the white meat
we all consumed in secret
before we were born
we shared the same meal.
When you impale me
upon your lances of narrow blackness
before you hear my heart speak
mourn your own borrowed blood
your own borrowed visions
Do not mistake my flesh for the enemy
do not write my name in the dust
before the shrine of the god of smallpox
for we are all children of Eshu
god of chance and the unpredictable
and we each wear many changes
inside of our skin.

Armed with scars
healed
in many different colors
I look in my own faces
as Eshu's daughter crying
if we do not stop killing
the other
in ourselves
the self that we hate
in others
soon we shall all lie
in the same direction
and Eshidale's priests will be very busy
they who alone can bury
all those who seek their own death
by jumping up from the ground
and landing upon their heads.

Future Promise

This house will not stand forever.
The windows are sturdy
but shuttered
like individual solutions
that match one at a time.

The roof leaks.
On persistent rainy days
I look up to see
the gables weeping
quietly.

The stairs are sound
beneath my children
but from time to time
a splinter leaves
imbedded in a childish foot.

I dream of stairways
sagging
into silence
well used and satisfied
with no more need
for changelessness

Once
freed from constancy
this house
will not stand
forever.

The Trollop Maiden

But my life is not portable now
said the trollop maiden
I need fixed light
to make my witless orchids
grow
into prizes
and the machine I use
to make my bread
is too bulky to move around
easily and besides
it needs
especially heavy current.

But the old maid who lives in your navel
is the trollop maiden's desire
and your orchids sing without smell
in the fixed light like sirens.

You can always run off
yourself
said the trollop maiden
but my life is not portable
yet she moved
into coquette with the rhythms
of a gypsy fiddle—
fired across my bow
with a mouthful of leaden pain
NOW
That's one piece I cannot leave behind
she whispered.

Solstice

We forgot to water the plantain shoots
when our houses were full of borrowed meat
and our stomachs with the gift of strangers
who laugh now as they pass us
because our land is barren
the farms are choked with stunted rows of straw
and with our nightmares
of juicy brown yams that cannot fill us.
The roofs of our houses rot from last winter's water
but our drinking pots are broken
we have used them to mourn the deaths of old lovers
the next rain will wash our footprints away
and our children have married beneath them.

Our skins are empty
They have been vacated by the spirits
who are angered by our reluctance
to feed them.
In baskets of straw made from sleep grass
and the droppings of civets
they have been hidden away by our mothers
who are waiting for us by the river.

My skin is tightening
soon I shall shed it
like a monitor lizard
like remembered comfort
at the new moon's rising
I will eat the last signs of my weakness
remove the scars of old childhood wars
and dare to enter the forest whistling
like a snake that has fed the chameleon
for changes
I shall be forever.

May I never remember reasons
for my spirit's safety
may I never forget

the warning of my woman's flesh
weeping at the new moon
may I never lose
that terror
that keeps me brave
May I owe nothing
that I cannot repay.

A Glossary of African Names
Used in the Poems

ABOMEY: The inland capital and heart of the ancient kingdom of Dahomey. A center of culture and power, it was also the seat of the courts of the Aladaxonu, the famed Panther Kings.

AKAI: Tight narrow braids of hair wrapped with thread and arranged about the head to form the elaborate coiffure of modern Dahomean high fashion.

AMAZONS: Unlike in other African systems of belief, women in Dahomey, as the Creators of Life, were not enjoined from the shedding of blood. The Amazons were highly prized, well-trained, and ferocious women warriors who guarded, and fought under the direction of, the Panther Kings of Dahomey.

ASEIN: Small metal altars upon high poles before which the deified ancestors are worshiped with offerings.

CONIAQUI: A West African people who occupy the area which is now part of Guinea and the Ivory Coast.

DAN: An ancient name for the kingdom of Dahomey (Danhomee).

ELEGBA, ELEGBARA, LEGBA: See ESHU.

ESHIDALE: A local *Orisha* of the Ife region in Nigeria, whose priests atone for and bury those who commit suicide by jumping up from the ground and falling upon their heads.

ESHU: Also known as Elegba in Dahomey and the New World. Eshu is the youngest and most clever son of Yemanjá (or of Mawulisa). The mischievous messenger between all the other *Orisha-Vodu* and humans, he knows their different languages and is an accomplished linguist who both transmits and interprets. This function is of paramount importance because the *Orisha* do not understand each other's language, nor the language of humans. Eshu is a prankster, also, a personification of all the unpredictable elements in life. He is often identified with the masculine principle, and his primary symbol is frequently a huge erect phallus. But Eshu-Elegba has no priests, and in many Dahomean religious rituals, his part is danced by a woman with an attached phallus. Because of his unpredictable nature, Eshu's shrines are built outside of every dwelling and village, and near every crossroads. He receives the first portion of any offering made to any other *Orisha-Vodu*, to help insure correct transmittal and a speedy answer.

FA: One's personal destiny—the personification of fate. This is also the name given to a widespread and elaborate metaphysical system of divination much used in Dahomey. Fa is sometimes called the writing of Mawulisa.

MAWULISA: Within the major pantheon of the *Vodu*, Mawulisa is the Dahomean female-male, sky-goddess-god principle. Sometimes called the first inseparable twins of the Creator of the Universe, Mawulisa (Mawu-Lisa) is also represented as west-east, night-day, moon-sun. More frequently, Mawu is regarded as the Creator of the Universe, and Lisa is either called her first son, or her twin brother. She is called the mother of all the other *Vodu*, and as such, is connected to the *Orisha* Yemanjá. (See also: SEBOULISA.)

ORISHA: The *Orisha* are the goddesses and gods—divine personifications—of the Yoruba peoples of Western Nigeria. As the Yoruba were originally a group of many different peoples with a similar language, there are close to six hundred *Orisha*, major and local, with greater or lesser powers, some overlapping.

The neighboring people of Dan, or Dahomey, as it came to be called, received many of their religious forms from the Yoruba, so many of the *Orisha* reappear with different names as Dahomean goddesses and gods, or *Vodu (Vodun)*. These *Orisha* frequently became the chief *Vodu* of a group of other natively Dahomean divine principles having similar powers and interests.

The *Orisha-Vodu* are divine, but not omnipotent. They are very powerful, but not always just. They are very involved in human affairs, and offerings must be made to maintain their good wishes. Many of the names and rituals of the *Orisha-Vodu* survive and flourish in religions practiced in Cuba, Brazil, Haiti, Grenada, and the United States. It is in Haiti and the United States that the religious traditions of Yoruba and Dahomey are most closely blended.

ORISHALA: A major *Orisha*, Orishala gives shape and form to humans in the womb before birth. His priests are in charge of burying women who die in pregnancy. He is sometimes also called Obatala, which means the God of Whiteness. (In the New World religions, Obatala is frequently female.) Those who are born crippled or deformed are under

Orishala's special protection. Some say these cripples and albinos were made purposely by the *Orisha* so that his worship would not be forgotten; others say that those deformed were errors fashioned during Orishala's drunkenness. Red palm oil and wine are taboo at his shrine, and the color white is sacred to him, as are all white foods.

SHANGO: One of Yemanjá's best-known and strongest sons, Shango is the *Orisha* of lightning and thunder, war, and politics. His colors are bright red and white, and his symbol is a two-headed axe. In Nigeria, the head of the Shango cult is frequently a woman, called the Alagba. In Dahomey, he is known as Hervioso, chief *Vodu* of the Thunder Pantheon.

SHOPONA: The *Orisha* of smallpox. He is the god of earth and growing things; the disease is considered the most severe punishment for those who break his taboos, or whose names are whistled near his shrine. Lesser punishments are measles and boils and other skin eruptions. He is very powerful and greatly feared. In Dahomey, he is called Sagbatá, and long before Jenner in Europe, Sagbatá's priests knew and practiced the principle of live vaccination, guarding it jealously.

SEBOULISA: The goddess of Abomey—"The Mother of us all." A local representation of Mawulisa, she is sometimes known as Sogbo, creator of the world. (See also: MAWULISA.)

YAA ASANTEWA: An Ashanti Queen Mother in what is now Ghana, who led her people in several successful wars against the British in the nineteenth century.

YEMANJÁ: Mother of the other *Orisha*, Yemanjá is also the goddess of oceans. Rivers are said to flow from her breasts. One legend has it that a son tried to rape her. She fled until she collapsed, and from her breasts, the rivers flowed. Another legend says that a husband insulted Yemanjá's long breasts, and when she fled with her pots he knocked her down. From her breasts flowed the rivers, and from her body then sprang forth all the other *Orisha*. River-smooth stones are Yemanjá's symbol, and the sea is sacred to her followers. Those who please her are blessed with many children.

Bibliography

Bascom, William. *The Yoruba of Southwestern Nigeria*. Holt, Rinehart & Winston. New York, 1969.

Courlander, Harold. *Tales of Yoruba Gods and Heroes*. Fawcett. Greenwich, Conn. 1973.

Herskovits, Melville. *Dahomey, Vols. I & II*. J. J. Augustin. New York. 1934.

Yoruba Temple. *The Gods of Africa*. Great Benin Books. New York. n.d.

CHOSEN POEMS
OLD AND NEW

(1982)

TO FRANCES LOUISE CLAYTON

our footsteps hold this place together
our decisions make the possible whole.

The Evening News

First rule of the road: attend quiet victims first.

I am kneading my bread Winnie Mandela
while children who sing in the streets of Soweto
are jailed for inciting to riot
the moon in Soweto is mad
is bleeding my sister into the earth
is mixing her seed with the vultures'
greeks reap her like olives out of the trees
she is skimmed like salt
from the skin of a hungry desert
while the Ganvie fisherwomen with milk-large breasts
hide a fish with the face of a small girl
in the prow of their boats.

Winnie Mandela I am feeling your face
with pain of my crippled fingers
our children are escaping their births
in the streets of Soweto and Brooklyn
(what does it mean
our wars
being fought by our children?)

Winnie Mandela our names are like olives, salt, sand
the opal, amber, obsidian that hide their shape well.
We have never touched shaven foreheads together
yet how many of our sisters' and daughters' bones
whiten in secret
whose names we have not yet spoken
whose names we have never spoken
I have never heard their names spoken.

*Second rule of the road: any wound will stop bleeding if
you press down hard enough.*

Za Ki Tan Ke Parlay Lot*

Oh za ki tan ke parlay lot
you who hear tell the others
there is no metaphor for blood
flowing from children
these are your deaths
or your judgments
za ki tan ke parlay lot
you who hear tell the others
this is not some other cities' trial
your locks are no protection
hate chips at your front doors like flint
flames creep beneath them
my children are resting in question
and your tomorrows flicker
a face without eyes
without future
za ki tan ke parlay lot
whose visions lie dead in the alleys
dreams bagged like old leaves
anger shorn of promise
you are drowning in my children's blood
without metaphor
oh you who hear tell the others
za ki tan ke parlay lot.

*Called in the streets of Carriacou, West Indies,
before a funeral or burial.

Afterimages

I

However the image enters
its force remains within
my eyes
rockstrewn caves where dragonfish evolve
wild for life, relentless and acquisitive
learning to survive
where there is no food
my eyes are always hungry
and remembering
however the image enters
its force remains.
A white woman stands bereft and empty
a black boy hacked into a murderous lesson
recalled in me forever
like a lurch of earth on the edge of sleep
etched into my visions
food for dragonfish that learn
to live upon whatever they must eat
fused images beneath my pain.

II

The Pearl River floods through the streets of Jackson
A Mississippi summer televised.
Trapped houses kneel like sinners in the rain
a white woman climbs from her roof to a passing boat
her fingers tarry for a moment on the chimney
now awash
tearless and no longer young, she holds
a tattered baby's blanket in her arms.
In a flickering afterimage of the nightmare rain
a microphone
thrust up against her flat bewildered words
  "we jest come from the bank yestiddy
    borrowing money to pay the income tax
    now everything's gone. I never knew
    it could be so hard."

Despair weighs down her voice like Pearl River mud
caked around the edges
her pale eyes scanning the camera for help or explanation
unanswered
she shifts her search across the watered street, dry-eyed
                "hard, but not this hard."
Two tow-headed children hurl themselves against her
hanging upon her coat like mirrors
until a man with ham-like hands pulls her aside
snarling "She ain't got nothing more to say!"
and that lie hangs in his mouth
like a shred of rotting meat.

      III
I inherited Jackson, Mississippi.
For my majority it gave me Emmett Till
his 15 years puffed out like bruises
on plump boy-cheeks
his only Mississippi summer
whistling a 21 gun salute to Dixie
as a white girl passed him in the street
and he was baptized my son forever
in the midnight waters of the Pearl.

His broken body is the afterimage of my 21st year
when I walked through a northern summer
my eyes averted
from each corner's photographies
newspapers protest posters magazines
Police Story, Confidential, True
the avid insistence of detail
pretending insight or information
the length of gash across the dead boy's loins
his grieving mother's lamentation
the severed lips, how many burns
his gouged out eyes
sewed shut upon the screaming covers
louder than life
all over

the veiled warning, the secret relish
of a black child's mutilated body
fingered by street-corner eyes
bruise upon livid bruise
and wherever I looked that summer
I learned to be at home with children's blood
with savored violence
with pictures of black broken flesh
used, crumpled, and discarded
lying amid the sidewalk refuse
like a raped woman's face.

A black boy from Chicago
whistled on the streets of Jackson, Mississippi
testing what he'd been taught was a manly thing to do
his teachers
ripped his eyes out his sex his tongue
and flung him to the Pearl weighted with stone
in the name of white womanhood
they took their aroused honor
back to Jackson
and celebrated in a whorehouse
the double ritual of white manhood
confirmed.

IV

"If earth and air and water do not judge them who are
we to refuse a crust of bread?"

Emmett Till rides the crest of the Pearl, whistling
24 years his ghost lay like the shade of a raped woman
and a white girl has grown older in costly honor
(what did she pay to never know its price?)
now the Pearl River speaks its muddy judgment
and I can withhold my pity and my bread.

"Hard, but not this hard."
Her face is flat with resignation and despair
with ancient and familiar sorrows

a woman surveying her crumpled future
as the white girl besmirched by Emmett's whistle
never allowed her own tongue
without power or conclusion
unvoiced
she stands adrift in the ruins of her honor
and a man with an executioner's face
pulls her away.

Within my eyes
the flickering afterimages of a nightmare rain
a woman wrings her hands
beneath the weight of agonies remembered
I wade through summer ghosts
betrayed by vision
hers and my own
becoming dragonfish to survive
the horrors we are living
with tortured lungs
adapting to breathe blood.

A woman measures her life's damage
my eyes are caves, chunks of etched rock
tied to the ghost of a black boy
whistling
crying and frightened
her tow-headed children cluster
like little mirrors of despair
their father's hands upon them
and soundlessly
a woman begins to weep.

[1981]

A Poem For Women In Rage

A killing summer heat wraps up the city
emptied of all who are not bound to stay
a black woman waits for a white woman
leans against the railing in the Upper Westside street
at intermission
the distant sounds of Broadway dim to lulling
until I can hear the voice of sparrows
like a promise I await
the woman I love
our slice of time
a place beyond the city's pain.

In the corner phonebooth a woman
glassed in by reflections of the street between us
her white face dangles
a tapestry of disasters seen
through a veneer of order
her mouth drawn like an ill-used roadmap
to eyes without core, a bottled heart
impeccable credentials of old pain.

The veneer cracks open
hate launches through the glaze into my afternoon
our eyes touch like hot wire
and the street snaps into nightmare
a woman with white eyes is clutching
a bottle of Fleischmann's gin
is fumbling at her waistband
is pulling a butcher knife from her ragged pants
her hand arcs backward "You Black Bitch!"
the heavy blade spins out toward me
slow motion
years of fury surge upward like a wall
I do not hear it
clatter to the pavement at my feet.

A gear of ancient nightmare churns
swift in familiar dread and silence

but this time I am awake, released
I smile. Now. This time is
my turn.
I bend to the knife my ears blood-drumming
across the street my lover's voice
the only moving sound within white heat
"Don't touch it!"
I straighten, weaken, then start down again
hungry for resolution
simple as anger and so close at hand
my fingers reach for the familiar blade
the known grip of wood against my palm
I have held it to the whetstone
a thousand nights for this
escorting fury through my sleep
like a cherished friend
to wake in the stink of rage
beside the sleep-white face of love

The keen steel of a dreamt knife
sparks honed from the whetted edge with a tortured shriek
between my lover's voice and the grey spinning
a choice of pain or fury
slashing across judgment like a crimson scar
I could open her up to my anger
with a point sharpened upon love.

In the deathland my lover's voice
fades
like the roar of a train derailed
on the other side of a river
every white woman's face I love
and distrust is upon it
eating green grapes from a paper bag
marking yellow exam-books tucked into a manilla folder
orderly as the last thought before death
I throw the switch.
Through screams of crumpled steel
I search the wreckage for a ticket of hatred
my lover's voice

calling
a knife at her throat.

In this steaming aisle of the dead
I am weeping
to learn the names of those streets
my feet have worn thin with running
and why they will never serve me
nor ever lead me home.
"Don't touch it!" she cries
I straighten myself
in confusion
a drunken woman is running away
down the Westside street
my lover's voice moves me
to a shadowy clearing.

Corralled in fantasy
the woman with white eyes has vanished
to become her own nightmare
a french butcher blade hangs in my house
love's token
I remember this knife
it carved its message into my sleeping
she only read its warning
written upon my face.

[1981]

October

Spirits
of the abnormally born
live on in water
of the heroically dead
in the entrails of snake.
Now I span my days like a wild bridge
swaying in place
caught between poems like a vise
I am finishing my piece of this bargain
and how shall I return?

Seboulisa, mother of power
keeper of birds
fat and beautiful
give me the strength of your eyes
to remember
what I have learned
help me to attend with passion
these tasks at my hand for doing.

Carry my heart to some shore
that my feet will not shatter
do not let me pass away
before I have a name
for this tree
under which I am lying.
Do not let me die
still
needing to be stranger.

[1980]

Sister, Morning Is A Time
For Miracles

A core of the conversations we never had
lies in the distance
between your wants and mine
a piece of each
buried beneath the wall that separates
our sameness
a talisman of birth
hidden at the root of your mother's spirit
my mother's furies.

Now reaching for you with my sad words
between sleeping and waking
a runic stone speaks
what is asked for is often destroyed
by the very words that seek it
like dew in the early morning
dissolving the tongue of salt as well as its thirst
and I call you secret names of praise and fire
that sound like your birthright
but are not the names of a friend
while you hide from me under 100 excuses
lying like tombstones along the road
between your house and mine.

I could accept any blame I understood
but picking over the fresh and possible loneliness
of this too-early morning
I find the relics of my history
fossilized into a prison
where I learn to make love forever
better than how to make friends
where you are encased like a half-stoned peach
in the rigid art of your healing
and in case you have ever tried to reach me
and I couldn't hear you

these words are in place of the dead air
still between us:

A memorial to conversations we won't be having
to laughter shared and important
as the selves we helped make real
but also to the dead
revelations we buried still-born
in the refuse of fear and silence
and your remembered eyes
which don't meet mine anymore.

(I never intended to let you slip through my fingers
nor to purchase your interest ever again
like the desire of a whore
who yawns behind her upturned hand
pretending a sigh of pleasure
and I have had that, too, already.)

Once I thought when I opened my eyes we would move
into a freer and more open country
where the sun could illuminate our different desires
and the fresh air do us honor for who we were
yet I have awakened at 4 A.M. with a ribald joke to tell you
and found I had lost the name of the street
where you hid under an assumed name
and I knew I would have to bleed again
in order to find you
but just once
in the possibilities of this too-early morning
I wanted you
to talk
not as a healer
but as a lonely woman
talking to a friend.

[1979]

Need: A Choral Of Black Women's Voices

for Patricia Cowan and Bobbie Jean Graham
and the Hundreds of Other Mangled Black Women
whose Nightmares Inform Them My Words

tattle tale tit
your tongue will be slit
and every little boy in town
shall have a little bit
    —nursery rhyme

I

  I: This woman is Black
      so her blood is shed into silence
      this woman is Black
      so her death falls to earth
      like the drippings of birds
      to be washed away with silence and rain.

  P.C.: For a long time after the baby came
      I didn't go out at all
      and it got to be really lonely.
      Then Bubba started asking about his father
      I wanted to connect with the blood again
      thought maybe I'd meet somebody
      and we could move on together
      help make the dream real.
      An ad in the paper said
      "Black actress needed
      to audition in a play by Black playwright."
      I was anxious to get back to work
      thought this might be a good place to start
      so on the way home from school with Bubba
      I answered the ad.
      He put a hammer through my head.

  B.J.G.: If you are hit in the middle of your body
      by a ten-ton truck
      your caved-in chest bears the mark of a tire

and your liver pops
like a rubber ball.
If you are knocked down by boulders
from a poorly graded hill
your dying is stamped by the rockprint
upon your crushed body
by the impersonal weight of it all
while life drips out through your liver
smashed by the mindless stone.
When your boyfriend methodically beats you to death
in the alley behind your apartment
and the neighbors pull down their windowshades
because they don't want to get involved
the police call it a crime of passion
not a crime of hatred
but I still died
of a lacerated liver
and a man's heel
imprinted upon my chest.

I: Dead Black women haunt the black maled streets
    paying the cities' secret and familiar tithe of blood
    burn blood beat blood cut blood
    seven year old child rape victim blood blood
    of a sodomized grandmother blood blood
    on the hands of my brother blood
    and his blood clotting in the teeth of strangers
    as women we were meant to bleed
    but not this useless blood
    my blood each month a memorial
    to my unspoken sisters falling
    like red drops to the asphalt
    I am not satisfied to bleed
    as a quiet symbol for no one's redemption
    why is it our blood
    that keeps these cities fertile?

    I do not even know all their names.
    My sisters deaths are not noteworthy
    nor threatening enough to decorate the evening news

not important enough to be fossilized
between the right-to-life pickets
and the San Francisco riots for gay liberation
blood blood of my sisters fallen in this bloody war
with no names no medals no exchange of prisoners
no packages from home
no time off for good behavior
no victories no victors

B.J.G.: Only us
kept afraid to walk out into moonlight
lest we touch our power
only us
kept afraid to speak out
lest our tongues be slit
for the witches we are
our chests crushed
by the foot of a brawny acquaintance
and a ruptured liver bleeding life onto the stones.

ALL: And how many other deaths
do we live through daily
pretending
we are alive?

II
P.C.: What terror embossed my face onto your hatred
what ancient and unchallenged enemy
took on my flesh within your eyes
came armed against you
with laughter and a hopeful art
my hair catching the sunlight
my small son eager to see his mother at work?
Now my blood stiffens in the cracks
of your fingers raised to wipe
a half-smile from your lips.
In this picture of you
the face of a white policeman
bends

over my bleeding son
decaying into my brother
who stalked me with a singing hammer.

B.J.G.: And what do you need me for, brother,
to move for you, feel for you, die for you?
You have a grave need for me
but your eyes are thirsty for vengance
dressed in the easiest blood
and I am closest.

P.C.: When you opened my head with your hammer
did the boogie stop in your brain
the beat go on
the terror run out of you like curdled fury
a half-smile upon your lips?
And did your manhood lay in my skull like a netted fish
or did it spill out like blood
like impotent fury off the tips of your fingers
as your sledgehammer clove my bone to let the light out
did you touch it as it flew away?

ALL: Borrowed hymns veil the misplaced hatred
saying you need me you need me you need me
like a broken drum
calling me black goddess black hope black strength
black mother
you touch me
and I die in the alleys of Boston
with a stomach stomped through the small of my back
a hammered-in skull in Detroit
a ceremonial knife through my grandmother's used vagina
my burned body hacked to convenience in a vacant lot
I lie in midnight blood like a rebel city
bombed into false submission
and our enemies still sit in power
and judgment
over us all.

P.C.: *I need you.*
    was there no place left
    to plant your hammer
    spend anger rest horror
    no other place to dig for your manhood
    except in my woman's brain?

B.J.G.: Do you need me submitting to terror at nightfall
    to chop into bits and stuff warm into plastic bags
    near the neck of the Harlem River
    and they found me there
    swollen with your need
    do you need me to rape in my seventh year
    till blood breaks the corners of my child's mouth
    and you explain I was being seductive

ALL: Do you need me to print on our children
    the destruction our enemies imprint upon you
    like a Mack truck or an avalanche
    destroying us both
    carrying home their hatred
    you are re-learning my value
    in an enemy coin.

III
    I: I am wary of need
        that tastes like destruction.
        I am wary of need that tastes like destruction.
        Who ever learns to love me
        from the mouth of my enemies
        walks the edge of my world
        like a phantom in a crimson cloak
        and the dreambooks speak of money
        but my eyes say death.

        The simplest part of this poem
        is the truth in each one of us
        to which it is speaking.
        How much of this truth can I bear to see
        and still live

unblinded?
How much of this pain
can I use?

ALL: *"We cannot live without our lives,"*
"We cannot live without our lives."

[1979]

Patricia Cowan, 21, bludgeoned to death in Detroit, 1978.

Bobbie Jean Graham, 34, beaten to death in Boston, 1979. One of 12 black women murdered within a 3-month period in that city.

"We cannot live without our lives" from a poem by Barbara Deming.

OUR DEAD BEHIND US

(1986)

to
Gloria I. Joseph
*tikoro nnko agyina**

* Ashanti proverb: "One head cannot go into counsel"

Sisters in Arms

The edge of our bed was a wide grid
where your fifteen-year-old daughter was hanging
gut-sprung on police wheels
a cablegram nailed to the wood
next to a map of the Western Reserve
I could not return with you to bury the body
reconstruct your nightly cardboards
against the seeping Transvaal cold
I could not plant the other limpet mine
against a wall at the railroad station
nor carry either of your souls back from the river
in a calabash upon my head
so I bought you a ticket to Durban
on my American Express
and we lay together
in the first light of a new season.

Now clearing roughage from my autumn garden
cow sorrel   overgrown rocket gone to seed
I reach for the taste of today
the *New York Times* finally mentions your country
a half-page story
of the first white south african killed in the "unrest"
Not of Black children massacred at Sebokeng
six-year-olds imprisoned for threatening the state
not of Thabo Sibeko, first grader, in his own blood
on his grandmother's parlor floor
Joyce, nine, trying to crawl to him
shitting through her navel
not of a three-week-old infant, nameless
lost under the burned beds of Tembisa
my hand comes down like a brown vise over the marigolds
reckless through despair
we were two Black women touching our flame
and we left our dead behind us
I hovered   you rose   the last ritual of healing
"It is spring," you whispered

"I sold the ticket for guns and sulfa
I leave for home tomorrow"
and wherever I touch you
I lick cold from my fingers
taste rage
like salt from the lips of a woman
who has killed too often to forget
and carries each death in her eyes
your mouth a parting orchid
"Someday you will come to *my* country
and we will fight side by side?"

Keys jingle in the door ajar   threatening
whatever is coming belongs here
I reach for your sweetness
but silence explodes like a pregnant belly
into my face
a vomit of nevers.

Mmanthatisi turns away from the cloth
her daughters-in-law are dyeing
the baby drools milk from her breast
she hands him half-asleep to his sister
dresses again for war
knowing the men will follow.
In the intricate Maseru twilights
quick   sad   vital
she maps the next day's battle
dreams of Durban   sometimes
visions the deep wry song of beach pebbles
running after the sea.

M-mán-tha-tisi: warrior queen and leader of the Tlokwa (Sotho) people
during the *mfecane* (crushing), one of the greatest crises in southern
African history. The Sotho now live in the Orange Free State, S. A.

Má-se-ru: scene of a great Tlokwa battle and now the capital of Lesotho

Durban: Indian Ocean seaport and resort area in Natal Province, S. A.

To the Poet Who Happens to Be Black and the Black Poet Who Happens to Be a Woman

I

I was born in the gut of Blackness
from between my mother's particular thighs
her waters broke upon blue-flowered lineoleum
and turned to slush in the Harlem cold
10 PM on a full moon's night
my head crested round as a clock
"You were so dark," my mother said
"I thought you were a boy."

II

The first time I touched my sister   alive
I was sure   the earth took note
but we were not new
false skin peeled off like gloves of fire
yoked flame   I was
stripped to the tips of my fingers
her song written into my palms my nostrils my belly
welcome home
in a language   I was pleased to relearn.

III

No cold spirit ever strolled through my bones
on the corner of Amsterdam Avenue
no dog mistook me for a bench
nor a tree   nor a bone
no lover envisioned my plump brown arms
as wings   nor misnamed me condor
but I can recall without counting
eyes
cancelling me out
like an unpleasant appointment
postage due
stamped in yellow   red   purple

any color
except Black   and choice
and woman
alive.

IV
I cannot recall the words of my first poem
but I remember a promise
I made my pen
never to leave it
lying
in somebody else's blood.

Outlines

I

What hue lies in the slit of anger
ample and pure as night
what color the channel
blood comes through?

A Black woman and a white woman
charter our courses close
in a sea of calculated distance
warned away by reefs of hidden anger
histories rallied against us
the friendly face of cheap alliance.

Jonquils through the Mississippi snow
you entered my vision
with the force of hurled rock
defended by distance and a warning smile
fossil tears   pitched over the heart's wall
for protection
no other women
grown beyond safety
come back to tell us
whispering
past the turned shoulders
of our closest
we were not the first
Black woman white woman
altering course to fit our own journey.

In this treacherous sea
even the act of turning
is almost fatally difficult
coming around full face
into a driving storm
putting an end to running
before the wind.

On a helix of white
the letting of blood
the face of my love
and rage
coiled in my brown arms
an ache in the bone
we cannot alter history
by ignoring it
nor the contradictions
who we are.

II
A Black woman and a white woman
in the open fact of our loving
with not only our enemies' hands
raised against us
means a gradual sacrifice
of all that is simple
dreams
where you walk the mountain
still as a water-spirit
your arms lined with scalpels
and I hide the strength of my hungers
like a throwing knife in my hair.

Guilt wove through quarrels like barbed wire
fights in the half forgotten schoolyard
gob of spit in a childhood street
yet both our mothers once scrubbed kitchens
in houses where comfortable women
died a separate silence
our mothers' nightmares
trapped into familiar hatred
the convenience of others drilled into their lives
like studding into a wall
they taught us to understand
only the strangeness of men.

To give   but not beyond what is wanted
to speak   as well as to bear
the weight of hearing
Fragments of the word wrong
clung to my lashes like ice
confusing my vision with a crazed brilliance
your face   distorted into grids
of magnified complaint
our first winter
we made a home outside of symbol
learned to drain the expansion tank together
to look beyond the agreed-upon disguises
not to cry each other's tears.

How many Februarys
shall I lime this acid soil
inch by inch
reclaimed through our gathered waste?
from the wild onion shoots of April
to mulch in the August sun
squash blossoms   a cement driveway
kale and tomatoes
muscles etch the difference
between I need and forever.

When we first met
I had never been
for a walk in the woods

   III
light catches two women on a trail
together   embattled by choice
carving an agenda with tempered lightning
and no certainties
we mark tomorrow
examining every cell of the past
for what is useful   stoked by furies
we were supposed to absorb by forty
still we grow   more precise with each usage

like falling stars or torches
we print code names upon the scars
over each other's resolutions
our weaknesses   no longer hateful.

When women make love
beyond the first exploration
we meet each other   knowing
in a landscape
the rest of our lives
attempts to understand.

IV

Leaf-dappled the windows lighten
after a battle that leaves our night in tatters
and we two glad to be alive   and tender
the outline of your ear pressed on my shoulder
keeps a broken dish from becoming always.

We rise to dogshit   dumped on our front porch
the brass windchimes from Sundance stolen
despair offerings of the 8 A.M. News
reminding us we are still at war
and not with each other
"give us 22 minutes and we will give you the world . . ."
and still we dare
to say we are committed
sometimes without relish.

Ten blocks down the street
a cross is burning
we are a Black woman and a white woman
with two Black children
you talk with our next-door neighbors
I register for a shotgun
we secure the tender perennials
against an early frost
reconstructing a future we fuel
from our living   different precisions

In the next room a canvas chair
whispers beneath your weight
a breath of you between laundered towels
the flinty places that do not give.

V

Your face upon my shoulder
a crescent of freckle over bone
what we share   illuminates what we do not
the rest is a burden of history
we challenge
bearing each bitter piece to the light
we hone ourselves upon each other's courage
loving
as we cross the mined bridge   fury
tuned like a Geiger counter

to the softest place.
One straight light hair on the washbasin's rim
difference
intimate as a borrowed scarf
the children arrogant as mirrors
our pillows' mingled scent
this grain of our particular days
keeps a fine sharp edge
to which I cling like a banner
in a choice of winds
seeking an emotional language
in which to abbreviate time.

I trace the curve of your jaw
with a lover's finger
knowing the hardest battle
is only the first
how to do what we need for our living
with honor and in love
we have chosen each other
and the edge of each other's battles
the war is the same

if we lose
someday women's blood will congeal
upon a dead planet
if we win
there is no telling.

Stations

Some women love
to wait
for life   for a ring
in the June light   for a touch
of the sun to heal them   for another
woman's voice   to make them whole
to untie their hands
put words in their mouths
form to their passages   sound
to their screams   for some other sleeper
to remember   their future   their past.

Some women want for their right
train   in the wrong station
in the alleys of morning
for the noon to holler
the night come down.

Some women wait for love
to rise up
the child of their promise
to gather from earth
what they do not plant
to claim pain for labor
to become
the tip of an arrow   to aim
at the heart of now
but it never stays.

Some women wait for visions
that do not return
where they were not welcome
naked
for invitations to places
they always wanted
to visit
to be repeated.

Some women wait for themselves
around the next corner
and call the empty spot peace
but the opposite of living
is only not living
and the stars do not care.

Some women wait for something
to change   and nothing
does change
so they change
themselves.

Equal Opportunity

The american deputy assistant secretary of defense
for Equal Opportunity
and safety
is a home girl.
Blindness slashes our tapestry to shreds.

The moss-green military tailoring sets off her color
beautifully
she says "when I stand up to speak in uniform
you can believe everyone takes notice!"
Superimposed skull-like across her trim square shoulders
dioxin-smear
the stench of napalm upon growing cabbage
the chug and thud of Corsairs in the foreground
advance like a blush across her cheeks
up the unpaved road outside Grenville, Grenada

An M—16 bayonet gleams
slashing away the wooden latch
of a one-room slat house in Soubise
mopping up   weapons search   pockets of resistance
Imelda   young   Black   in a tattered headcloth
standing to one side on her left foot
takes notice
one wrist behind her hip the other
palm-up beneath her chin   watching
armed men in moss-green jumpsuits turn out her shack
watching   mashed-up nutmeg trees
the trampled cocoa pods
graceless broken stalks of almost ripe banana
her sister has been missing now ten days

Beside the shattered waterpipe downroad
Granny Lou's consolations
       If it was only kill
       they'd wanted to kill we

> many more would have died
> look at Lebanon
> so as wars go this was an easy one
> But for we here
> who never woke up before
> to see plane shitting fire into chimney
> it was a damn awful lot!

The baby's father buried without his legs
burned bones in piles along the road
"any Cubans around here, girl? any guns?"
singed tree-ferns curl and jerk in the mortar rhythms
strumming up from shore   uphill a tree explodes
showering the house with scraps of leaves
the sweetish smell of unseen rotting flesh.

For a while there was almost enough
water   enough rice   enough quinine
the child tugs at her waistband
but she does not move quickly
she has heard how nervous these green men are
with their grenades and sweaty helmets
who offer cigarettes and chocolate but no bread
free batteries and herpes but no doctors
no free buses to the St. Georges market
no reading lessons in the brilliant afternoons
bodies strewn along Telescope Beach
these soldiers say are foreigners
but she has seen the charred bits of familiar cloth
and knows what to say to any invader
with an M—16 rifle held ready
while searching her cooking shed
overturning the empty pots with his apologetic grin
Imelda steps forward
the child pressing against her knees
"no guns, man, no guns here. we glad you come. you carry
water?"

The american deputy assistant secretary of defense
for equal opportunity and safety

pauses in her speech   licks her dry lips
"as you can see the Department has
a very good record
of equal opportunity for our women"
swims toward safety
through a lake of her own blood.

Soho Cinema

The woman who lives at 830 Broadway
walks her infant at twilight
through the neighborhood streets
warehoused   fashionably ugly
200-dollar silk blouses where hammers once hung
between the cafés and loading docks
chemicals bloom like wild roses in the gutter
her child in the tattersall pram
with an anti-nuclear sticker
takes it all in as possible
in an urban parlor.

Does she promise her daughter a life
on this island   easier   safer
than the ones they rush home to peruse
26 stories up over a bay
that is dying
the complex
double-crostic of this moment's culture?

When the six o'clock news is over
does the child pat her mother's wet cheeks
does she cradle her daughter against her
and weep for what she has seen
beside the bed under which they are lying
deathstink in the mattress
her son bayonetted to the door in Santiago de Chile
a corolla of tsetse flies crusting her daughter's nose
army hippos fire into the mourners
across Bleecker Street
blood on her Escoffier knives
blood welling in her garbage disposal
her baby's blood obscuring the screen
their next decade in living color
wired from pole to pole
when the six o'clock news is over
does she weep for what she has seen?

Or does she will her orange rebozo
with the Soho magenta fringe
to a Vieques campesina
six children and no land left
after the mortars
and the Navy
sailing into the sunset.

Vigil

Seven holes in my heart where flames live
in the shape of a tree
upside down
bodies hang in the branches
Bernadine selling coconut candy
on the war-rutted road to St. Georges
my son's bullet-proof vest
dark children
dripping off the globe
like burned cheese.

Pale early girls spread themselves
handkerchiefs in the grass
near willow
a synchronized throb of air
swan's wings are beating
strong enough to break a man's leg
all the signs say
do not touch.

Large solid women
walk the parapets beside me
mythic   hunted
knowing
what we cannot remember
hungry   hungry
windfall
songs at midnight
prepare me for morning.

Berlin Is Hard on Colored Girls

Perhaps a strange woman
walks down from the corner
into my bedroom
wasps nest behind her ears
she is eating a half-ripe banana
with brown flecks in the shape of a lizard
kittiwakes in her hair
her armpits smell of celery
perhaps
she is speaking my tongue
in a different tempo
the rhythm of gray whales praying
dark as a granite bowl
perhaps
she is a stone.

I cross her borders at midnight
the guards confused by a dream
Mother Christopher's warm bread
an end to war   perhaps
she is selling a season's ticket to the Berlin Opera
printed on the lid of a dim box
slowing the growth of rambler roses
perhaps   ice-saints have warned us
the tender forgiveness of contrasts
metal   silken thighs   a beached boat
perhaps   she is masquerading
in the american flag
in the hair-bouncing step
of a jaunty flower-bandit
perhaps
A nightingale waits in the alley
next to the yellow phone booth
under my pillow
a banana skin is wilting.

This Urn Contains Earth from German Concentration Camps

Plotzensee Memorial, West Berlin, 1984

Dark gray
the stone wall hangs
self-conscious wreaths
the heavy breath of gaudy Berlin roses
"The Vice Chancellor Remembers
The Heroic Generals of the Resistance"
and before a well-trimmed hedge
unpolished granite
tall as my daughter and twice around
Neatness
wiping memories   payment
from the air.

Midsummer's Eve beside a lake
keen   the smell of quiet
children straggling homeward
rough precisions of earth
beneath my rump
in a hollow root of the dead elm
a rabbit kindles.

The picnic is over
reluctantly
I stand   pick up my blanket
and flip into the bowl of still-warm corn
a writhing waterbug
cracked open   her pale eggs oozing
quiet
from the smash.

Earth
not the unremarkable ash
of fussy thin-boned infants

and adolescent Jewish girls
liming the Ravensbruck potatoes
careful and monsterless
this urn makes nothing
easy to say.

Mawu

In this white room full of strangers
you are the first face of love   remembered
but I belong to myself in the rude places
in the glare of your angriest looks
your blood   running through my dreams
like red angry water
and whatever I kill
turns in the death grasp
into your last   most beautiful
silence.

Released
from the prism of dreaming
we make peace with the women
we shall never become
I measured your betrayals
in a hundred different faces
to claim you as my own
grown cool   and delicate   and grave
beyond revision

So long as your death is a leaving
it will never be my last.

Departure sounds bell through the corridor
I rise and take your hand
remembering   beyond denials
I have survived
the gifts   still puzzling me
as in the voice of my departing mother
antique and querulous
flashes of old toughness   shine through like stars
teaching me how to die   insisting
death is not a disease.

Fishing the White Water

Men claim the easiest spots
stand knee-deep in calm dark water
where the trout is proven.

I never intended to press beyond
the sharp lines set as boundary
named as the razor names
parting the skin
and seeing the shapes of our weaknesses
etched into afternoon
the sudden vegetarian hunger for meat
tears on the typewriter
tyrannies of the correct
we offer mercy   forgiveness
to ourselves and our lovers
to the failures we underline daily
insisting upon next Thursday
yet forgetting to mention each other's name
the mother of desires
wrote them under our skin.

I call the stone   sister   who remembers
somewhere my grandmother's hand
brushed   on her way to market
to the ships
you can choose   not to live
near the graves where your grandmothers sing
in wind through the corn.

There have been easier times
for loving   different richness
if it were only the stars
we had wanted
to conquer
I could turn from your dear face
into the prism light makes
along my line

we cast into rapids
alone   back to back
laboring the current.

In some distant summer
working our way farther from bone
we will lie in the river
silent as caribou
and the children will bring us food.

You carry the yellow tackle box
a fishnet over your shoulder
knapsacked
I balance the broken-down rods
our rhythms pass through the trees
staking a claim   in difficult places
we head for the source.

On the Edge

A blade in the bed of a child
will slice up nightmare
into simpler hungers.

But a knife is a dangerous gift
girl brave enough to be crazy
you may never read this poem again
so commit it   like sin
or a promise   to the place
where poetry arms your beauty
with a hundred knives
some mined in the hills above Whydah
for a good looking Creek
on the run.

The rhythms of your long body
do not yet move in my blood
but the first full moon of this year
is a void of course moon
I dream   I am precious rock
touching   the edge of you
that needs
the moon's loving.

Naming the Stories

Otter and quaking aspen
the set of a full cleansing moon
castle walls crumble
in silence
visions trapped by the wild stone
lace up the sky   pale electric fire
no sound
but a soft expectation of birds
calling the night home.

Half asleep   bells
mark a butterfly's birth
over the rubble
I crawl into dawn
corn woman bird girl sister
calls from the edge of a desert
where it is still night
to tell me her story
survival.

Rock speaks   a rooster language
and the light is broken
clear.

Diaspora

Afraid is a country with no exit visas
a wire of ants walking the horizon
embroiders our passports at birth
Johannesburg Alabama
a dark girl flees the cattle prods
skin hanging from her shredded nails
escapes into my nightmare
half an hour before the Shatila dawn
wakes in the well of a borrowed Volkswagen
or a rickety midnight sleeper out of White River Junction
Washington bound   again
gulps carbon monoxide in a false-bottomed truck
fording the Braceras Grande
or an up-country river
grenades held dry in a calabash
leaving.

The Horse Casts a Shoe

The horse casts a shoe
edged cobbles are speaking
the journey ends in a wood
metal remains.

On the path
light catches two women upon a trail
heat rises like mist from the skin
unsaddled
the sacred and different
stretches to muscled limit
two women tremble
the spotty light trembles
limbs of hemlock weaving a shelter
above us
I tremble your season
unshod against mine.

We enter a landscape
seize likeness   lie down together
a horseshoe's clatter still ringing
our bodies bridged across terror
our names
a crostic for touch.

Reins

Refuse the meat of a female animal
when you are bearing
or her spirit may turn against you
and your child   fall in the blood.

Do not cook fish with bulging eyes
nor step over running water
the spirits of streams are restless
and can pull your child down and away.

Do not joke with your grandfather
if you wish many strong children
nor hunt rabbits   in the afternoon

From the eighth day
when the child is named
to keep your milk flowing
do not eat coconut
after the sun goes down.

Wood Has No Mouth

When a mask breaks in Benin
the dancer must fast
make offerings
as if a relative died.

The mask cannot speak
the dancer's tears
are the tears of a weeping spirit.

Brown grain   mute
as a lost detail
Thoth
goddess of wisdom
disguised
as a baboon.

A Meeting of Minds

In a dream
she is not allowed
dreaming
the agent of control is
a zoning bee
her lips are wired to explode
at the slightest conversation
she stands
in a crystal
all around
other women are chatting
the walls are written in honey
in the dream
she is not allowed
to kiss her own mother
the agent of control
is   a white pencil
that writes
alone.

The Art of Response

The first answer was incorrect
the second was
sorry   the third trimmed its toenails
on the Vatican steps
the fourth went mad
the fifth
nursed a grudge until it bore twins
that drank poisoned grape juice in Jonestown
the sixth   wrote a book about it
the seventh
argued a case before the Supreme Court
against taxation on Girl Scout Cookies
the eighth held a news conference
while four Black babies
and one other   picketed New York City
for a hospital bed to die in
the ninth and tenth swore
Revenge on the Opposition
and the eleventh dug their graves
next to Eternal Truth
the twelfth
processed funds from a Third World country
that provides doctors for Central Harlem
the thirteenth
refused
the fourteenth sold cocaine and shamrocks
near a toilet in the Big Apple circus
the fifteenth
changed the question.

From the Cave

Last night an old man warned me
to mend my clothes
we would journey before light
into a foreign tongue.
I rode down autumn
mounted on a syllabus
through stairwells hung in dog
and typewriter covers
the ocean is rising
father
I came on time
and the waters touched me.

A woman I love
draws me
a bath of old roses.

A Question of Climate

I learned to be honest
the way I learned to swim
dropped into the inevitable
my father's thumbs in my hairless armpits
about to give way
I am trying
to surface   carefully
remembering
the water's shadow-legged musk
cannons of salt   exploding
my nostrils' rage
and for years
my powerful breast stroke
was a declaration of war.

Out to the Hard Road

The road to Southampton is layered with days
in different directions
you   driving an ecru sedan
through potato dust velvet   asphalt
beyond Patchogue   Yaphank   Ronkonkoma
and one of us always gave in
at the Center Moriches turn
the road narrows down to a sudden thirst
and Sally twirls her famed lemons
one eye out for the boys in blue.

Part of our secret lay hidden
in Monday's pocket   for comfort
we always go back
to our graves.

I never told you how much it hurt   leaving
casting myself adrift like a wounded ship
not the sharp edge of alone   kills
but no seen ending to over
reluctance   lining my mouth
potato dust   on the last shortcut
out
to a new September morning.

Every Traveler Has
One Vermont Poem

Spikes of lavender aster under Route 91
hide a longing or confession
"I remember when air was invisible"
from Chamberlin Hill down to Lord's Creek
tree mosses point the way home.

Two nights of frost
and already the hills are turning
curved green against the astonished morning
sneeze-weed and ox-eye daisies
not caring   I am a stranger
making a living choice.

Tanned boys I do not know
on their first proud harvest
wave from their father's tractor
one smiles as we drive past
the other hollers
nigger
into cropped and fragrant air.

For Judith

Hanging out
means being
together
upon the earth
boulders
crape myrtle trees
fox and deer
at the watering hole
not quite together
but learning
each other's ways.

For Jose and Regina

Children of war
learn
to grow up alone
and   silently
hoping
no one will notice
somebody's life could depend on it.

Children of war
know
the worst times
come announced
by a disagreeable whine
mother's rage   always
relieved
by a definite reason.

Beverly's Poem

I don't need to be rich
just able
to know how it feels
to get bored
with anemones.

Big Apple Circus

"Most of us out here don't think about
New York at all except as a zoo"

Used to be
the circus was for rich kids
every week in summer
I went by subway to the Bronx Zoo
Thursday was free day
the mandrill
scowling menace over his shoulder
shoves his crimson rump
into a nightmare now
grim tigers prowl shelved rock
tired of weeping.

The circus is a promise
silver dresses made of music
well-trained grins in a gaudy trick
the elephants' painted feet
that will not stamp out fools
nor advance to battle
up the Battery   across Maiden Lane
storming the Staten Island Ferry
clowns dive into nets that sing
and answer back
even the rifles fire flowers
but no bread
there are circuses in Pretoria
Moscow   Eau Claire   Alabama
soon there may even be a circus on the moon.

Between the acts
in littered alleys
tourists look like mourners
come to change their clothes
The seductive music hints
no more funeral marches
and we cannot hear the guns
across the river.

Florida

Black people fishing the causeway
full-skirted   bare brown to the bellyband
atilt on the railing   near a concrete road
where a crawler-transporter will move
the space shuttle from hangar to gantry.

Renting a biplane to stalk the full moon in Aquarius
as she rose under Venus between propellers Country Western surf
feasting on frozen black beans Cubano from Grand Union
in the mangrove swamp   elbows of cypress   scrub oak

Moon   moon   moon on the syncopated road
rimey with bullfrogs   walking beaches   fragrant and raunchy
fire-damp sand between my toes.

Huge arrogant cockroaches   with white people's manners
and their palmetto bug cousins
aggressive ridged slowness
the obstinacy of living fossils.

Sweet ugly-fruit   avocados   tomatoes
and melon in the mango slot
hibiscus spread like a rainbow of lovers
arced stamens waving
but even the jacaranda only last a day.

Crescent moon walking my sheets at midnight
lonely in the palmetto thicket   counting
persistent Canaveral lizards launch themselves
through my air conditioner
chasing equally determined fleas.

In Gainesville the last time there was only one
sister present who said   "I'm gonna remember your name
and the next time you come there'll be
quite a few more of us, hear?"
and there certainly was   a warm pool

of dark women's faces
in the sea of listening.

The first thing I did when I got home
after kissing my honey
was to wash my hair with small flowers
and begin a five-day fast.

Home

We arrived at my mother's island
to find your mother's name in the stone
we did not need   to go to the graveyard
for affirmation
our own genealogies
the language of childhood wars.

Two old dark women
in the back of the Belmont lorry
bound for L'Esterre
blessed us   greeting
Eh Dou-Dou you look *too* familiar
to you   to me
it no longer mattered.

Burning the Water Hyacinth

We flame the river
to keep the boat paths open
your eyes eat my shadow
at the light line
touchless
completing   each other's need
to yearn
to settle into hunger
faceless
a waning moon.

Plucking desire
from my palms
like the firehairs of a cactus
I know this appetite
the greed of a poet
or an empty woman
trying to touch
what matters.

Political Relations

In a hotel in Tashkent
the Latvian delegate from Riga
was sucking his fishbones
as a Chukwu woman with hands as hot as mine
caressed my knee beneath the dinner table
her slanted eyes were dark as seal fur
we did not know each other's tongue.

"Someday we will talk through our children"
she said
"I spoke to your eyes this morning
you have such a beautiful face"
thin-lipped Moscow girls translated for us
smirking at each other.

And I had watched her in the Conference Hall
ox-solid   black electric hair
straight as a deer's rein   fire-disc eyes
sweeping over the faces
like a stretch of frozen tundra
we were two ends of one taut rope
stretched like a promise from her mouth
singing the friendship song
her people sang for greeting
> There are only fourteen thousand of us left
> it is a very sad thing   it is a very sad thing
> when any people   any people   dies

"Yes, I heard you this morning"
I said   reaching out from the place where we touched
poured her vodka   an offering
which she accepted like roses
leaning across our white Russian interpreters
to kiss me softly upon my lips.

Then she got up and left
with the Latvian delegate from Riga.

Learning to Write

Is the alphabet responsible
for the book
in which it is written
that makes me peevish and nasty
and wish I were dumb   again?

We practiced drawing our letters
digging into the top of the desk
and old Sister Eymard
rapped our knuckles
until they bled
she was the meanest of all
and we knew she was crazy
but none of the grownups
would listen to us
until she died in a madhouse.

I am a bleak heroism of words
that refuse
to be buried alive
with the liars.

On My Way Out I Passed Over You and the Verrazano Bridge

Leaving   leaving
the bridged water
beneath
the red sands of South Beach
silhouette houses sliding off the horizon
oh love,   if I become anger
feel me
holding you in my heart circling
the concrete   particular
arcs of this journey
landscape of trials
not to be lost in choice   nor decision
in the nape of the bay
our house slips under these wings
shuttle between nightmare and the possible.

The broad water drew us, and the space
growing enough green to feed ourselves over two seasons
now sulfur fuels burn in New Jersey
and when I wash my hands at the garden hose
the earth runs off bright yellow
the bridge disappears
only a lowering sky
in transit.

So do we blow the longest suspension bridge in the world
up from the middle
or will it be bombs at the Hylan Toll Plaza
mortars over Grymes Hill
flak shrieking through the streets of Rosebank
the home of the Staten Island ku klux klan
while sky-roaches napalm the Park Hill Projects
we live on the edge
of manufacturing
tomorrow or the unthinkable
made common as plantain-weed

by our act of not thinking
of taking
only what is given.

       Wintry Poland survives
       the bastardized prose of the *New York Times*
       while Soweto is a quaint heat treatment
       in some exotic but safely capitalized city
       where the Hero Children's bones moulder unmarked
       and the blood of my sister in exile Winnie Mandela
       slows   and her steps slow
       in a banned and waterless living
       her youngest daughter is becoming a poet.

I am writing these words as a route map
an artifact for survival
a chronicle of buried treasure
a mourning
for this place we are about to be leaving
a rudder for my children   your children
our lovers   our hopes   braided
from the dull wharves of Tompkinsville
to Zimbabwe   Chad   Azania
oh Willie sweet little brother with the snap in your eyes
what walls are you covering now
with your visions of revolution
the precise needs of our mother earth
the cost of false bread
and have you learned to nourish your sisters at last
as well as to treasure them?

       Past darkened windows of a Bay Street Women's Shelter
       like ghosts through the streets of Marazan
       the northeastern altars of El Salvador
       move the belly-wise blonded children of starvation
       the once-black now wasted old people
       who built Pretoria
       Philadelphia   Atlanta   San Francisco
       and even ancient London—yes, I tell you
       Italians owned Britain

and Hannibal blackened the earth from the Alps to the Adriatic
Roman blood sickles like the blood of an African people
so where is true history written
except in the poems?

I am inside the shadow dipped upon your horizon
scanning a borrowed *Newsweek* where american soldiers
train seven-year-old Chilean boys
to do their killing for them.

Picture small-boned dark women
gun-belts taut over dyed cloth
between the baby and a rifle
how many of these women
activated plastique near the oil refineries
outside Capetown
burned their houses behind them
left
the fine-painted ochre walls
the carved water gourds still drying
and the new yams not yet harvested
which one of these women
was driven out of Crossroads
perched on the corrugated walls of her uprooted life
strapped to a lorry
the cooking pot banging her ankles
which one
saw her two-year-old daughter's face
squashed like a melon
in the pre-dawn police raids upon Noxolo
which one   writes poems
lies with other women
in the blood's affirmation?

History is not kind to us
we restitch it with living
past memory   forward
into desire
into the panic   articulation

of want   without having
or even the promise of getting.

And I dream of our coming together
encircled   driven
not only by love
but by lust for a working tomorrow
the flights of this journey
mapless   uncertain
and necessary as water.

Out of the Wind

to Blanche

For the days when the coffee grounds refuse to settle
and the last toothpick rolls into a crack on the floor
and all the telephone messages are from enemies
or for other people only
and the good old days
lie
between pages of books
we have already written
for the acorn of fear in each April
will this be the year
earth refuses
to forgive us with a blush of green
for the weary assumptions
of next winter's chill
and for silent days inbetween
your face
mingled in tulips
after brief rain.

Holographs

One hundred and fifty million truth seekers
at the trough of the evening news
arteries bumping and writhing
against Pik Botha's belly
a keg of sound
and how does it feel
to bury this baby you nursed for a year
weighing less than when she was born?

60,000 Pondo women keening
on the mountain
the smell of an alley in Gugeleto
after the burned bodies are dragged through
pennywhistles and stickdrum beats
earth under the high—arched feet
of deadly exuberant children
stones in their kneepants pockets
running toward Johannesburg
some singing   some waving
some stepping to intricate patterns
their fathers knew   tomorrow
they will be dead.

How can I mourn these children
my mothers and fathers
their sacred generous laughter
the arms' bright marrow
willow shadows upon the stair
Young men do not dream of dying
they seek the taut sinew
pulled   the passions of use
a latch slid into place
in the cold flickering light
the only dependable warmth
is the burn of the blood.

There Are No Honest Poems
About Dead Women

What do we want from each other
after we have told our stories
do we want
to be healed   do we want
mossy quiet stealing over our scars
do we want
the powerful unfrightening sister
who will make the pain go away
mother's voice   in the hallway
you've done it right
the first time   darling
you will never need
to do it again.

Thunder grumbles on the horizon
I buy time with another story
a pale blister of air
cadences of dead flesh
obscure the vowels.

A Question of *Essence*

In Arlesheim
the solstice smelled like hair pomade
the moon
caught between warm and forever
I dream of Alice Walker
her tears on my shoulder
but I cannot see her face
dark women painted clay pale
dash in and out of laughter
clay in their eyes   in their ears
around their noses
their tongues bedded down in clay
some are building shelters
against the past
low huts of seductive pictures
other beautiful women
Is Your Hair Still Political?
tell me
when it starts to burn . . .

For the Record

in memory of Eleanor Bumpers

Call out the colored girls
and the ones who call themselves Black
and the ones who hate the word nigger
and the ones who are very pale

Who will count the big fleshy women
the grandmother weighing 22 stone
with the rusty braids
and a gap-toothed scowl
who wasn't afraid of Armageddon
the first shotgun blast tore her right arm off
the one with the butcher knife
the second blew out her heart
through the back of her chest
and I am going to keep writing it down
how they carried her body out of the house
dress torn   up around her waist
uncovered
past tenants and the neighborhood children
a mountain of Black Woman
and I am going to keep telling this
if it kills me
and it might in ways I am
learning

The next day Indira Gandhi
was shot down in her garden
and I wonder what these two 67-year-old
colored girls
are saying to each other now
planning their return
and they weren't even
sisters.

Ethiopia

for Tifa

Seven years without milk
means everyone dances for joy
on your birthday
but when you clap   your hands
break at the wrist
and even grandmother's ghee
cannot mend
the delicate embroideries
of bone.

Generation III

Give back the life I gave
you   pay me my money down
so there's no question
I did it for love   for anything
but desire
put a tarnished nickel in my dish
so the guard will know
when he comes
with a bleeding chicken
tied to his wrist
with a bitter promise
that we are not kin
uncommitted forever.

Pay me what you cannot afford
to relinquish in rush hour streets
impaled on the high heels of women
jiggling and sweet
and tough as witches in a vineyard
where even your sweat smells
like love.

In the playground
children's voices are singing
Rise Africa You Will Be Free
a grown woman
steps over my rigid legs
stretched across the threshold of a kitchen
where pink and blue cakes cool in the window
on alternate days
you cradle me
dab lard on my right cheek
where the key to our house
burned a scar
the shape of your new name
in the enemy's tongue.

Never to Dream of Spiders

Time collapses between the lips of strangers
my days collapse into a hollow tube
soon implodes against now
like an iron wall
my eyes are blocked with rubble
a smear of perspectives
blurring each horizon
in the breathless precision of silence
one word is made.

Once the renegade flesh was gone
fall air lay against my face
sharp and blue as a needle
but the rain fell through October
and death lay   a condemnation
within my blood.

The smell of your neck in August
a fine gold wire bejeweling war
all the rest lies
illusive as a farmhouse
on the other side of a valley
vanishing in the afternoon.

Day three   day four   day ten
the seventh step
a veiled door leading to my golden anniversary
flameproofed free-paper shredded
in the teeth of a pillaging dog
never to dream of spiders
and when they turned the hoses upon me
a burst of light.

Beams

In the afternoon sun
that smelled of contradiction
quick birds announcing spring's intention
and autumn about to begin
I started to tell you
what Eudora never told me
how quickly it goes
the other fork   out of mind's eye
choice
becoming a stone wall
across possible
beams
outlined on the shapes of winter
the sunset colors of Southampton Beach
red-snapper runs at Salina Cruz
and we slept in the fishermen's nets
a pendulum swing
between the rippling fingers
of a belly dancer with brass rings
and a two-year-old's sleep smell
the inexorable dwindling
no body's choice
and for a few short summers
I too was delightful.

Whenever spring comes I wish to burn
to ride the flood like a zebra goaded
shaken with sun
to braid the hair of a girl long dead
or is it my daughter grown
and desire for what is gone
sealed into hunger like an abandoned mine
nights when fear came down like a jones
and I lay rigid with denials
the clarity of frost without
the pain of coldness

autumn's sharp precisions and yet
for the green to stay.

Dark women clad in flat and functional leather
finger their breastsummers whispering
sisterly advice one dreams of fish
lays her lips like spring across my chest
where I am scarred and naked
as a strip-mined hill in West Virginia
and hanging on my office wall
a snapshot of the last Dahomean Amazons
taken the year that I was born
three old Black women in draped cloths
holding hands.

A knout of revelation   a corm of song
and love   a net of possible
surrounding all acts of life
one woman harvesting   all I have ever been
lights up my sky like stars
or flecks of paint   storm-flung
the blast and seep of gone
remains
only the peace we make with it
shifts into seasons
lengthening past equinox
sun   wind   come round again
seizing us in her arms like a warrior lover
or blowing us into shapes
we have avoided for years
as we turn
we forget what is not possible.

_____

A jones: a drug habit or addiction.

Breastsummer: a breastplate; also a wooden beam across an
empty place.

416

Call

Holy ghost woman
stolen out of your name
Rainbow Serpent
whose faces have been forgotten
Mother   loosen my tongue or adorn me
with a lighter burden
Aido Hwedo is coming.

On worn kitchen stools and tables
we are piecing our weapons together
scraps of different histories
do not let us shatter
any altar
she who scrubs the capitol toilets, listening
is your sister's youngest daughter
gnarled Harriet's anointed
you have not been without honor
even the young guerrilla has chosen
yells as she fires into the thicket
Aido Hwedo is coming.

I have written your names on my cheekbone
dreamed your eyes   flesh my epiphany
most ancient goddesses   hear me
enter
I have not forgotten your worship
nor my sisters
nor the sons of my daughters
my children watch for your print
in their labors
and they say Aido Hwedo is coming.

I am a Black woman   turning
mouthing your name as a password
through seductions   self-slaughter
and I believe in the holy ghost
mother

in your flames beyond our vision
blown light through the fingers of women
enduring   warring
sometimes outside your name
we do not choose all our rituals
Thandt Modise   winged girl of Soweto
brought fire back home in the snout of a mortar
and passes the word from her prison cell   whispering
Aido Hwedo is coming.

Rainbow Serpent who must not go
unspoken
I have offered up the safety of separations
sung the spirals of power
and what fills the spaces
before power unfolds or flounders
in desirable nonessentials
I am a Black woman   stripped down
and praying
my whole life has been an altar
worth its ending
and I say Aido Hwedo is coming.

I may be a weed in the garden
of women I have loved
who are still
trapped in their season
but even they shriek
as they rip burning gold from their skins
Aido Hwedo is coming.

We are learning by heart
what has never been taught
you are my given   fire-tongued
Oya   Seboulisa   Mawu   Afrekete
and now we are mourning our sisters
lost to the false hush of sorrow
to hardness and hatchets and childbirth
and we are shouting
Rosa Parks and Fannie Lou Hamer

Assata Shakur and Yaa Asantewa
my mother and Winnie Mandela are singing
in my throat
the holy ghosts' linguist
one iron silence broken
Aido Hwedo is calling
calling
your daughters are named
and conceiving
Mother   loosen my tongue
or adorn me
with a lighter burden
Aido Hwedo is coming.

Aido Hwedo is coming.

Aido Hwedo is coming.

Aido Hwedo: The Rainbow Serpent; also a representation of all
ancient divinities who must be worshipped but whose names and
faces have been lost in time.

THE MARVELOUS ARITHMETICS OF DISTANCE

(1993)

To My Sister Pat Parker, Poet and
Comrade-in-Arms In Memoriam

and to my blood sisters
Mavis Jones
Marjorie Jones
Phyllis Blackwell
Helen Lorde

Smelling the Wind

Rushing headlong
into new silence
your face
dips on my horizon
the name
of a cherished dream
riding my anchor
one sweet season
to cast off
on another voyage

No reckoning allowed
save the marvelous arithmetics
of distance

Legacy—Hers

When love leaps from my mouth
cadenced in that Grenada wisdom
upon which I first made holy war
then I must reassess
all my mother's words
or every path I cherish.

Like everything else I learned from Linda
this message hurtles across still uncalm air
silent   tumultuous   freed water
descending an imperfect drain.

I learn how to die
from your many examples
cracking the code of your living
heroisms   collusions   invisibilities
constructing my own
book of your last hours
how we tried to connect
in that bland spotless room
one bright Black woman
to another   bred for endurance
for battle

> *island women make good wives*
> *whatever happens they've seen worse . . .*

your last word to me was   *wonderful*
and I am still seeking the rest
of that terrible acrostic

Making Love to Concrete

An upright abutment in the mouth
of the Willis Avenue bridge
a beige Honda leaps the divider
like a steel gazelle   inescapable
sleek leather boots on the pavement
rat-a-tat-tat   best intentions
going down for the third time
stuck   in the particular

You cannot make love to concrete
if you care about being
non-essential   wrong or worn   thin
if you fear ever becoming
diamonds or lard
you cannot make love to concrete
if you cannot pretend
concrete needs your loving

To make love to concrete
you need an indelible feather
white dresses before you are ten
a confirmation lace veil   milk-large bones
and air raid drills in your nightmares
no stars till you go to the country
and one summer when you are twelve
Con Edison pulls the plug
on the street-corner moons   Walpurgisnacht
and there are sudden new lights in the sky
stone chips that forget   you need
to become a light rope   a hammer
a repeatable bridge
garden-fresh broccoli   two dozen dropped
     eggs
and a hint of you

caught up between my fingers
the lesson of a wooden beam
propped up on barrels
across the mined terrain

between forgiving too easily
and never giving at all.

Echoes

There is a timbre of voice
that comes from not being heard
and knowing   you are not being
heard   noticed only
by others   not heard
for the same reason.

The flavor of midnight fruit   tongue
calling your body through dark light
piercing the allure of safety
ripping the glitter of silence
around you
      dazzle me with color
      and perhaps I won't notice
till after you're gone
your hot grain smell tattooed
into each new poem   resonant
beyond escape   I am listening
in that fine space
between desire and always
the grave stillness
before choice.

As my tongue unravels
in what pitch
will the scream hang unsung
or shiver like lace on the borders
of never   recording
which dreams heal   which
dream can kill
stabbing a man and burning his body
for cover   being caught
making love to a woman
I do not know.

Domino

On Thursday she buried her featherbed
at the foot of the garden
a Manx cat's bleached pelvic bone
twirled in the sun.

She had never intended to stay
so long   horizons burning
past forsythia   bracken
all roads out of her dooryard
folded in
upon reflection.

Every full moon
the neighborhood cats
came to worship
to wait   in a grim line
under the apple tree
the cat-bone swings
to a heavy beat

Sharpeville
Amritsar
Shatila
Birmingham Sunday

Imagine yourself
alabama
wanting to weep.

Thaw

The language of past seasons
collapses   pumpkins in spring
false labor slides like mud
off the face of ease
and whatever I turn my hand to
pales in the sun.

We will always be there to your call
the old witches said
always said   always saying
something else   at the same time
you are trapped   asleep
you are speechless
perhaps   you will also be
broken.

Step lightly   all around us
words are cracking
off   we drift
separate and syllabic
if we survive at all.

Party Time

Newspapers printed in secret report
bent needles under the child's fingernail
barbed stitches through the bleeding scalp
grandchildren playing hide and seek
riddled with bullets behind a silk-cotton tree
just two more funerals in Soweto
behind the small coffins
Lillian's son-in-law drags his feet
achilles tendons shredded by police dogs
festering   in their eyes
each memory of home
poised over potshards in the dawn.*

But who sings the song
of my mothers' muscled beauty
these large sore-bodied women
with nimble tongues   gnarled ankles
stepping to an elegant rhythm
arms akimbo in quick march time
rocking with laughter   and the young ones
strut   without illusion
weathered extreme bodies
blossom   in the singing night
Lillian's hooded eyes invite me
into the circle   a strum of voices
weaving an intricate drum.

Over grapejuice in South Provence
the women from South Africa
lower their voices   discussing rents
and who has not yet paid   a protest
punishable by death
burning through the Mofolo night.

*Potshards left on a woman's hearthstone are a sign one
  of her sons did not survive an initiation rite.

Eleanor Bumpurs, grandmother,
shotgunned
against her kitchen wall
by rent marshals in the Bronx
moves among us   humming
her breath is sweet acacia
in this stone yard at sunset
rhythms quicken
and I come next   behind her
in our dance.

Prism

for Joyce Serote

There are no frogs in Soweto
students croak
Amandla! through the tear-gas.

Not true no frogs live in Soweto
only we are too weary
with no ears left to hear them.

Who knows where frogs live in Soweto
who has time to listen
stroll along a moonlit gutter
beyond the flames of evening
rising   falling
the thin high screams
of skewered children.

In the bruising fist of challenge
the future does not tarry.

Take our words to bed with you
dream upon them
choose any ones you wish
write us a poem.

Do You Remember Laura

Alive
between the Panther News and Zabar's
an Upper West Side proper
exiled to Brooklyn
where she became a style
Broadway in the winter and the rain
long fingers flashing
Red Zinger tea at Teacher's
next to Bolton's
piperack elegance.

One unguarded turn
from curb to never
the car leaps my control
like an adolescent girl
one hand against the windshield
in surprise   another
saying no   I did not choose this
death   I want my say.

Forgive me Laura
I could have been your lover
in time longing skids   crashes
but does not self-destruct.

433

Inheritance—His

I

My face resembles your face
less and less each day. When I was young
no one mistook whose child I was.
Features   build   coloring
alone among my creamy fine-boned sisters
marked me Byron's daughter.

No sun set when you died, but a door
opened onto my mother. After you left
she grieved her crumpled world aloft
an iron fist sweated with business symbols
a printed blotter   *dwell in a house of Lord's*
your hollow voice chanting down a hospital corridor
                yea, though I walk through the valley
                of the shadow of death
                I will fear no evil.

II

I rummage through the deaths you lived
swaying on a bridge of question.
At seven   in Barbados
dropped into your unknown father's life
your courage vault from his tailor's table
back to the sea
Did the Grenada treeferns sing
your 15th summer as you jumped ship
to seek your mother
finding her   too late
surrounded with new sons?

Who did you bury to become enforcer of the law
the handsome legend
before whose raised arm even trees wept
a man of deep and wordless passion
who wanted sons and got five girls?
You left the first two scratching in a treefern's shade

the youngest is a renegade poet
searching for your answer in my blood.

My mother's Grenville tales
spin through early summer evenings.
But you refused to speak of home
of stepping proud Black and penniless
into this land where only white men
ruled by money.   How you labored
in the docks of the Hotel Astor
your bright wife a chambermaid upstairs
welded love and survival to ambition
as the land of promise withered
crashed   the hotel closed
and you peddle dawn-bought apples
from a pushcart on Broadway.
Does an image of return
wealthy and triumphant
warm your chilblained fingers
as you count coins in the Manhattan snow
or is it only Linda
who dreams of home?

When my mother's first-born crys for milk
in the brutal city winter
do the faces of your other daughters dim
like the image of the treeferned yard
where a dark girl first cooked for you
and her ash heap still smells curry?

III
Did the secret of my sisters steal your tongue
like I stole money from your midnight pockets
stubborn and quaking
as you threaten to shoot me if I am the one?
the naked lightbulbs in our kitchen ceiling
glint off your service revolver
as you load   whispering.

Did two little dark girls in Grenada
dart like flying fish
between your averred eyes
and my pajamaless body
our last adolescent summer
eavesdropped orations
to your shaving mirror
our most intense conversations
were you practicing how to tell me
of my twin sisters   abandoned
as you had been abandoned
by another Black woman seeking
her fortune   Grenada   Barbados
Panama   Grenada.
New York City.

   IV

You bought old books at auction
for my unlanguaged world
gave me your idols   Marcus Garvey   Citizen Kane
and morsels from your dinner plate
when I was seven.
I owe you my Dahomeyan jaw
the free high school for gifted girls
no one else thought I should attend
and the darkness that we share.
Our deepest bonds remain
the mirror and the gun.

   V

An elderly Black judge
known for his way with women
visits this island where I live
shakes my hand, smiling
"I knew your father," he says
"quite a man!" Smiles again.
I flinch at his raised eyebrow.
A long-gone woman's voice
lashes out at me   in parting

"You will never be satisfied
until you have the whole world
in your bed!"

Now I am older than you were when you died
overwork and silence exploding in your brain.
You are gradually receding from my face.
Who were you outside the 23rd Psalm?
Knowing so little
how did I become so much
like you?

Your hunger for rectitude
blossoms into rage
the hot tears of mourning
never shed for you before
your twisted measurements
the agony of denial
the power of unshared secrets.

[January 23–September 10, 1992]

The One Who Got Away

The youngest sister
works a dangerous ground
mildewed   combustible
beyond glamour or choice
she is last seen
leaping the dangerous pegmatite
under noon's mercy.

Each day she lives
a bright ransom
going away   beyond the guilty
cut to the border   evening
hounds baying across the clearing.

Each day a new landscape
but never a woman
peeks out from the folds
of her bed-scented mirror
to whisper   you are the fairest
daughter.

And every midnight
over her nightmare's shoulder
a swollen girl
belly pressed against glass
waves goodbye
through the slanting rain.

Depreciation

Staten Island, 1986

First the plumbing breaks down
a minor valve slips with a hiss
as the first guests sit down
amontillado in hand.

Between the leek soup and curried flounder
an era begins in the basement
the furnace gives up
its castiron forevers   slowly
the pump stutters   groans
refusing to move
we promise each other
future celebrations.

Syracuse Airport

Clean jeans and comfortable shoes
I need no secrets here   at home
in this echoless light
I spread my papers out
around me.

Opposite   alert
a grey-eyed lady takes fire
one pale nostril quivering
we both know women
who take up space
are called sloppy.

Thanks to Jesse Jackson

January 1, 1989

The US and the USSR
are/were the most powerful countries
in the world
but only $\frac{1}{8}$ of the world's population.
African people are also $\frac{1}{8}$ of the world's population.
$\frac{1}{2}$ of the world's people are Asian.
$\frac{1}{2}$ of that number is Chinese.

There are 22 nations in the Middle East.

So most people in this world
are Yellow, Black, Brown, Poor, Female
Non-Christian
and do not speak english.

By the year 2000
the 20 largest cities in the world
will have two things in common
none of them will be in Europe
and none in the United States.

Judith's Fancy

Half-built
your greathouse looms
between me and the sun.
Shell-smells on the morning wind.
You are younger than my daughter
the boy you hold is blond
the moon is new.
My sloping land brings our eyes level
"Welcome, neighbor," I begin.

Were we enemies in another life
or do your eyes always turn to flint
when meeting a Black woman
face to face?

Your child speaks first.
"I don't like you," he cries
"Are you coming to babysit me?"

Production

100,000 bees make a sturdy hive
ready   three days after the moon is
    full
we cut honey.

Our hot knives slice the caps of wax
from each heavy frame
dark pollened richness drips
from the laden combs.

Sadiq loads the extractor
Curtis leveling the spin.
Sweet creeps like bees
through each crack of hot air.

Outside the honey house
hungry drones cluster
low-voiced and steady
we strain the flow   laughing
drunk with honey.

Before twilight
long rows of bottles stand
labeled and waiting.

Tomorrow we make a living
two dollars at a time.

Building

Gloria has a permit
to change the earth
plucks flies
from the air
while discussing
revolution
is taken for local
in a lot
of different places.

jessehelms

I am a Black woman
writing my way to the future
off a garbage scow knit from moral fiber
stuck together with jessehelms'
come   where Art is a dirty word
scrawled on the wall
of Bilbo's memorial outhouse
and obscenity is catching
even I'd like to hear you scream
ream out your pussy
with my dildo called Nicaragua
ram Grenada up your fighole
till Panama runs out of you
like Savimbi aflame.

But you prefer to do it
on the senate floor
amid a sackful of paper pricks
keeping time to a 195 million dollar
military band
safe-sex dripping from your tongue
into avid senatorial ears.

Later you'll get yours
behind the senate toilets
where they're waiting for you jessehelms
those white boys with their pendulous rules
bumping against the rear door of Europe
spread-eagled across the globe
their crystal balls poised over Africa
ass-up for old glory.

Your turn now jessehelms
come on its time
to lick the handwriting
off the walls.

Dear Joe

if you have ever tried to reach me
and I could not hear you
these words are in place of the dead air
still between us.
   —"Morning Is a Time for Miracles"

How many other dark young men at 33
left their public life   becoming legend
the mysterious connection
between whom we murder
and whom we mourn?

Everyone here likes our blossoms
permanent
and the flowers around your casket
will never die
preserved without error
in the crystals between our lashes
they will never bang down the phone
in our jangled ears at 3:30 A.M.
nor call us to account for our silence
nor refuse to answer
or say get away from me
this is my way   or say
we are wrong   prejudiced   lazy
deluded   cowardly   insignificant   faint
or say fuck you seven times in one sentence
when the circumstance of our lives
becomes so chaotic
words fly away like drunken buzzards
or say we might fail   or say
we might fail but that's no reason
to stop   to miss a beat
and the tinny jukebox music
comes up through the floor of our shoes.

Nobody here will lean too heavily
on your flowers
nor lick the petals of the lavender gladiola

for a hint of sweetness
wilting it with a whiskey blast
threatening the faint-hearted
with a handshake or a bottle of beer.

In the side pews   always ghosts
who resemble
our brothers   past and future
who say they were also our lovers   but they lie
terror caught in their throats like a lump of clay
and the taxi is waiting to take them back
out to the sunshine.

A pale refugee from a nameless country
hawks wired roses from stool to stool
down the street
at the Pathmark Pharmacy
a drag-queen with burgundy long-johns
and a dental dam in his mouth
is buying a straight razor.

Women on Trains

for Jacqui and Angela

Leaving the known for another city
the club-car smells of old velvet
rails whisper relief mantras
steel upon steel
every fourth thud breaks the hum
"stand and fight," I said
leaving my words for ransom
"your only way out."

This train is a doorway
bent into the shape of a scale.

Eleanor Roosevelt riding the rails
behind her husband's casket
forefinger tense along a propped cheek
one knuckle caressing her lips
young Nell's dreams strung along
sentinel stalks of mullein
giving
in the whip of the journey's wind
my mother's mandatory hat
at a no-nonsense tilt
beside the tenement windows of wartime
scanning Lenox Avenue
for a coal-delivery truck.

Women on trains
have a life
that is exactly livable
the precision of days flashing past
no intervention allowed
and the shape of each season
relentlessly carved in the land.

I have soared over crannied earth
spread like a woman waiting

but this angled sky anchors me
inward   through the ugliness
shards of bright fireweed   loosestrife
and stacks of heat-treated lumber   beyond
the bare arms of scrub-maple and poplar
already ablush.

Was it ever business as usual for these women
as snow-driven hopes and fears swirled
past tenement office windows
and nappy-topped stands of unreachable trees
flowed along in the southern dusk?

The coal truck arrived after dark   dumping
barely half-a-ton of bituminous
my father gone to his second job
she shoveled it down herself
in the freezing Harlem night
and coal dusted my mother's tired hat
as the subway screamed us home.

Women on trains have a chance
to unweave their tangles.
Perhaps between Blythe and Patchoula
Eleanor chose to live her own days.
The subway tunnel walls
closed in like thunder
and my mother never had a chance
to lay her magic down.

Between new lumber and the maples
I rehear your question
owning
the woman who breaks   the woman
who is broken.

I counseled you unwisely my sister
to be who I am   no longer
willing to be for my living
stopgap   hurled into the breach

beyond support   beyond change
and I search these rushing sun-dark trees
for your phone number
to acknowledge
both you and I
are free to go.

The Politics of Addiction

17 luxury condominiums
electronically protected
from criminal hunger   the homeless
seeking a night's warmth
across from the soup kitchen
St. Vincent's Hospital
razor wire covering the hot air grates.
Disrobed need
shrieks through the nearby streets.

Some no longer beg.
a brown sloe-eyed boy
picks blotches from his face
eyes my purse shivering
white dust a holy fire
in his blood
at the corner   fantasy
parodies desire   replaces longing
Green light.   The boy turns back
to the steaming grates.

Down the street in a show-window
camera   Havana
the well-shaped woman smiles
waves her plump arm along
half-filled market shelves
excess expectation
dusts across her words
"Si hubieran capitalismo
hubiesen tomates aquí!"
"If we had capitalism
tomatoes would be here now."

Kitchen Linoleum

The cockroach
who is dying
and the woman
who is blind
agree
not to notice
each other's shame.

Oshun's Table

Amsterdam, 1986

How the fruit lay at your feet
how you dressed the wine
cut green beans
in a lacy network
wound to the drum
russet arm hairs
in the candlelight
we ate pom and fish rice
with a fork and spoon.

A short hard rain
and the moon came up
before we lay down together
we toasted each other
descendants of poets
and woodcutters
handsome
untrustworthy
and brave.

Parting

I talk to rocks
sometimes they answer
double-voiced
as a woman in love
taking leave
in roars of jade.

Carnelian promises an end to bleak
through secret eyes of malachite
I look toward obsidian
to absolve my dreaming.

The jasper-red stone
in the gizzard of swallows
heals the moon-touched
the poor   and the disagreeable.

But it refuses to be taken
leaps off the sideboard
out of my loving fingers
hurls itself from the prow
of a borrowed canoe

And the swirling adventurine water
chants a coral   carved
with your moon-rock's name.

Peace on Earth

Christmas, 1989

A six-pointed star
in the eyes of a Polish child
lighting her first shabbas candle   fading
into a painted cross on the Berlin Wall
gnarled Lithuanian hands at prayer
Romania's solemn triumph
a dictator's statue ground into dust
(SINTI-What?)*

Before the flickering screen
goes dead   rows of erupting houses
the rockets' red glare   where
are all these brown children
running scrambling around the globe
flames through the rubble
bombs bursting in air
Panama   Nablus   Gaza
tear gas clouding the Natal sun.

THIS IS A GIFT FROM THE PEOPLE
OF THE UNITED STATES OF AMERICA[†]
quick cut
the crackling Yule Log
in an iron grate.

---

* Sinti-Roma: the correct name for the still oppressed so-
  called Gypsy people of Romania.

[†] Stamped in large print on all emergency food packages
  sent to conquered countries.

Restoration: A Memorial—9/18/91

Berlin again   after chemotherapy
I reach behind me once more
for days to come
sweeping around the edges of authenticity
two years after Hugo blew one life away
Death like a burnt star
perched on the rim of my teacup
flaming the honey drips from my spoon
sunlight flouncing off the gargoyles opposite.

Somewhere it is Tuesday
in the ordinary world
ravishment fades
into compelling tasks
our bodies learn to perform
quite a bit of the house is left
our bedroom spared
except for the ankle-deep water
and terrible stench.

Would I exchange this safety of exile
for the muddy hand-drawn water
wash buckets stashed
where our front porch had been
half-rotten vegetables
the antique grey settling over your face
that October?

I want you laughing again
After the stinking rugs are dragged away
the crystal chandelier dug
from the dining-room floor
refrigerator righted
broken cupboards stacked outside
to dry for our dinner fire.

A few trees still stand
in a brand-new landscape
but the sea road is impassable.
Your red shirt
hung out on a bush to dry
is the only flower for weeks.
No escape. No return.
No other life
half so sane.

In this alien and temporary haven
my poisoned fingers
slowly return to normal
I read your letter dreaming
the perspective of a bluefish
or a fugitive parrot
watch the chemicals leaving my nails
as my skin takes back its weaknesses.
Learning to laugh again.

Starting All Over Again

January 1, 1992

It's great to be able to call you
at strange hours of my night
asking you to explain
yourself   wondering
if that land you approach
radar in hand
climbing an unknown sea
where sailors dare not go lightly
is my face   your grandfather's
broad-lipped island face
so like mine
is your own face.

It is not wrong to hunger
for a cause   till the need
burns upriver
to your heart   becomes
an unquenchable taste
only you must believe
yourself
and the power to choose
your own selves
your best campaign.

I believe in you my son
and I tremble
but the whole earth is trembling
and no one is talking
more than 100,000 dead bodies
in the strange land between us
and still no word spoken
but you share my sleep
with a Kuwaiti girl
impaled twice
by the sprouting hatred of a conqueror
whose face is hidden from me

and by her brother
who loathes the child she bears.

Dark incandescent winds blow
the belch of smoldering oil wells
around the world
dimming my island sunsets
mingling with the black smoke
of Ellen Goodman's son
aflame on the Amherst green.

In one month I celebrate
the beginning of my second Saturn return
you were the gift of my first
and I trust you   beyond question

In what do you believe?

What It Means to Be Beautiful

The child believes
what she sees
becomes her own
each morning   over toothpaste
in front of the mirror
another woman's mouth
goes tight as a zipper.

On the night wall
desire hangs
Virgin   unattainable
a tiny white woman smiling
the perfect fantasy of my sister
chains the door she opens
to wave me goodbye
admitting no common air
no debt to our morning.

I stumble over her threshold
razor wire   under the clothesline
I am scolded for inattention
lick where the iron flavor wells
hide   an unbitten star-apple
melting to sludge in my palm.

Hugo I

A coral stone at the edge of Bufano Road
where the storm sat down
but did not sleep
the jack pine I used to curse
for its ragged outline
as the evening shadows walked
across yucca stumps
where quits perched all last summer
fussing their yellow song.

A grey dog lay in the road
pregnant with death
as I planted new bougainvillea
that fortnight Gloria went North.

This skeleton was an almond tree.
That stalk a prickly pear cactus
green as a gourd
a peep of red fruit
promised and warned
in the same sticky breath.

All the rest is rubble.
Constructions
that fester and grow loathsome
because they cannot self-destruct.
In some fantasy of immortality
a wilted wisdom formed them
to last 10,000 years.

But the wind is our teacher.

Construction

Timber seasons better
if it is cut in the fourth quarter
of a barren sign.

In Cancer
the most fertile of skysigns
I shall build a house
that will stand forever.

Speechless

At the foot of the steps a forest
strewn with breadcrumb fingers
sticky with loss
stuffed with seductive chaotic songs
like a goose bound for the oven
giddy trees wait   shaken.

In the wild arms of a twilit birch
the void of course moon
hangs like a spotlit breast.

Death
folds the corners of my mouth
into a heart-shaped star
sits on my tongue like a stone
around which your name blossoms
distorted.

For Craig

If I call you son and not brother
it is because I pray
my son learns your conceit   your daring
who came so late   and left too soon
If I call you brother and not son
it is to mourn my own loss
that my mother did not live long enough
to bear you.

You said we should always be brave
and I try to be   every morning
over my toothbrush and the waning stars
I peer through your eyes
through your taut heart's muscle
beating war rhythms
with determination
and a brush of bells.

East Berlin

It feels dangerous now
to be Black in Berlin
sad suicides that never got reported
Neukölln   Kreuzberg   the neon Zoo
a new siege along Unter den Linden
with Paris accents   New York hustle
many tattered visions intersecting.

Already my blood shrieks
through East Berlin streets
misplaced hatreds
volcanic tallies rung upon cement
Afro-German woman stomped to death
by skinheads in Alexanderplatz
two-year-old girls
half-cooked in their campcots
who pays the price
for their disillusion?

Hand-held the candles wink
in Berlin's scant November light
hitting the Wall at 30 miles an hour
vision first
is still hitting a wall
and on the other side
the rank chasm
where dreams of laurels lie
hollowness wed to triumph
differing from defeat
only in the approaching tasks.

The Night-Blooming Jasmine

Lady of the Night   star-breathed
blooms along the searoad
between my house and the tasks before me
calls down a flute
carved from the legbone of a gull.

Through the core of me
a fine rigged wire
upon which pain will not falter
nor predict
I was no stranger to this arena
at high noon
beyond was not an enemy
to be avoided
but a challenge
against which my neck grew strong
against which my metal struck
and I rang like fire in the sun.

I still patrol that line
sword drawn
lighting red-glazed candles of petition
along the scar
the surest way of knowing
death is a fractured border
through the center of my days.

Bees seek their need
until flowers beckon
beyond the limit of their wings
then they drop where they fly
pollen baskets laden
the sweet work done.

They do not know the Lady of the Night
blossoms
between my house and the searoad

calling down a flute
carved from the legbone of a gull
your rich voice
riding the shadows of conquering air.

[November 1990–May 1992]

Girlfriend

March 27, 1990

It's almost a year and I still
can't deal with you
not being
at the end of the line.

I read your name in memorial poems
and think they must be insane
mistaken   malicious
in terrible error
just plain wrong

not that there haven't been times before
months passing   madly   sadly
we not speaking
      get off my case, will you please?
      oh, just lighten up!

But I can't get you out
of my air   my spirit
my special hotline phone book
is this what it means to live
forever   when will I
not miss picking up the receiver
after a pregnancy of silence
one of us born again
with a brand-new address or poem
miffed
because the other doesn't jump
at the sound
of her beloved voice?

Lunar Eclipse

August 16, 1989

Last night I watched the moon go out
become a dark opalescent glow
I could not believe what was happening
even as I saw the change in light.

The first time I met you
we sat up all night reading
each other's poems   morning hopes
followed us down Cole Street
chattering like a flock of quits.

You stretch across our best years
like a living wire
between heaven and hell
at war   Being sisters
wasn't always easy
but it was never dull.

I can't believe you are gone
out of my life
So you are not.

Change

In whose bed
did I lie asweat
as the first thrush sounded
telling myself stories
of someone I used to be
hurling myself
at the unfamiliar shore
taunting the rocks' long shadow
till the waves beat my rage
back to spindrift
and my wars came home?

The girls who live
at the edge of the calm pool
where the moon rises
teach me
to leave dreams alone.

Today Is Not the Day

I can't just sit here
staring death in her face
blinking and asking for a new name
by which to greet her

I am not afraid to say
unembellished
I am dying
but I do not want to do it
looking the other way.

Today is not the day.
It could be
but it is not.
Today is today
in the early moving morning
sun shining down upon
the farmhouse in my belly
lighting the wellswept alleys
of the town growing in my liver
intricate vessels swelling with the gift
of Mother Mawu
or her mischievous daughter
Afrekete Afrekete   my beloved
feel the sun of my days surround you
binding our pathways
we have water to carry
honey to harvest
bright seed to plant for the next fair
we will linger
exchanging sweet oil
along each other's ashy legs
the evening light
a crest on your cheekbones.

By this rising
some piece of our labor

is already half-done
the taste of loving
doing a bit of work
having some fun
riding my wheels so close to the line
my eyelashes blaze.

Beth dangles her stethoscope over the rearview mirror
Jonathan fine-tunes his fix on Orion
working through another equation
youth taut as an arrow
stretched to their borders
the barb sinking in so far
it vanishes from the surface.
I dare not tremble for them
only pray laughter comes often enough
to soften the edge.

And Gloria   Gloria
whose difference I learn
with the love of a sister   you   you
in my eyes bright appetite   light
playing along your muscle
as you swing.

This could be the day.
I could slip anchor and wander
to the end of the jetty
uncoil into the waters
a vessel of light   moonglade
ride the freshets to sundown
and when I am gone
another stranger will find you
coiled on the warm sand
beached treasure   and love you
for the different stories
your seas tell
and half-finished blossoms

growing out of my season
trail behind
with a comforting hum.

But today
is not the day.
Today.

[April 22, 1992]

The Electric Slide Boogie

New Year's Day 1:16 A.M.
and my body is weary beyond
time to withdraw and rest
ample room allowed me in everyone's head
but community calls
right over the threshold
drums beating through the walls
children playing their truck dramas
under the collapsible coatrack
in the narrow hallway outside my room

The TV lounge next door is wide open
it is midnight in Idaho
and the throb   easy   subtle   spin
of the electric slide boogie
step-stepping
around the corner of the parlor
past the sweet clink
of dining room glasses
and the edged aroma of slightly overdone
dutch-apple pie
all laced together
with the rich dark laughter
of Gloria
and her higher-octave sisters

How hard it is to sleep
in the middle of life.

[January 3, 1992]

INDEX

Poems with more than one page reference indicate revised versions.

Y